Runner's World

ADVANCED RUNNING BOOK

Runner's World

ADVANCED RUNNING BOOK

by Cordner Nelson

Runner's World Books

Library of Congress Cataloging in Publication Data

Nelson, Cordner.
   Runner's world advanced running book.

   1. Running–Training. I. Runner's world. II. Title. III. Title: Advanced running book.

GV1061.5.N44   1983   796.4'26   83-13721

ISBN: 0-89037-273-X

Photo Credits

*Robert Gerloff p. 127; David Keith p. 87 ; David Madison p. 122;
Horst Muller p. 105; Stan Pantovic p. 125; Jeff Reinking pp. 98, 123;
Mark Shearman pp. 41, 119, 132; Andy Whipple p. 75.*

ANDERSON WORLD BOOKS, INC.
1400 Stierlin Road
Mountain View, CA, 94043

printed in U.S.A.

Contents

Dedication 7

Introduction 9

PART ONE: PRINCIPLES OF TRAINING 11

1 Who Should Run, and Why 13

2 Stress: How Your Body Adapts 19

3 How to Train for Aerobic Endurance 23

4 Strength Training 56

5 Speed Training 69

6 Combining Speed with Endurance 78

7 The Energy Formula 89

8 Combination Training 101

PART TWO: TRAINING FOR YOUR SPECIAL EVENT 107

9 Training According to Distance 108

10 Skill Development 117

PART THREE: YOUR TRAINING PROGRAM 133

11 Endurance First 134

12 Strength Next 143

13 The Anaerobic and Speed Phase 146

14 Managing Your Competitive Season 152

15 The Big Race 156

PART FOUR: HOW TO RACE 161

16 Competitive Effort 162

17 Conserving Energy 172

References 183

Dedication

To Sarah, Ellen and David.

Introduction

If you want to improve as a runner, your choice of training methods is vital. Your choice may be 1) scientific, 2) empirical, or 3) Gedanken:

1. Scientific research is responsible for several training systems, notably Gerschler's interval training. On the other hand, scientists have arrived at some amusing conclusions based on research that fails to see the whole picture. To choose a training method based entirely upon science would be as foolish as to ignore scientific evidence.

2. Empirical evidence is the kind you get from experience or observation. This undoubtedly accounts for well over 90 percent of the training methods used during the history of distance running, as runners copied the methods of the most successful. It has been a history of trial and error with many false leads, because some highly talented runners succeeded with less than perfect training. Still, this nearly blind learning mill has gradually narrowed its focus and now approaches closer to perfection.

3. Gedanken is a German term used in physics. It means you can reach truths by thinking, the best example being Einstein's Theory of Relativity. This sort of theorizing has led to Arthur Lydiard's use of hill training, Mihaly Igloi's speed training, altitude running, work with weights and, of course, many refinements to the methods of other runners.

Obviously, your best chance to approach the perfect training routine is to use all three methods. To do so requires a knowledge of basic physiology, and so this book begins with a study of how your body reacts to various training methods. If you understand physiology, you'll understand training.

After you have gained understanding, you must apply it to yourself. Unlike many training books, this one assumes there is no single, perfect method. You are different from every other runner, and so you must seek the methods best for you. What's more, you need different methods for different parts of the year, probably for different years and, sometimes, you must change your plan for a single day.

You may never find the perfect training method. It is possible no runner will ever find it. But you *can* improve your present methods. Whether you are a 1:45 800-meter runner or a four-hour marathoner, this book can help you improve if you will study and apply the art and science of training.

PART ONE:

PRINCIPLES OF TRAINING

1

Who Should Run, and Why

What do these people have in common?:

1. A three-year-old girl leaves her mother and runs awkwardly across the lawn, smiling with joy.

2. A 43-year-old housewife jogs through the park in her multicolored running shoes.

3. A skinny 15-year-old boy tries to keep up with the pack in a cross-country race, hoping to make the B team. His name is Jim Ryun.

4. A 29-year-old teacher walks toward the starting line with his wife, two children, and a picnic basket, and he greets his competitors with real pleasure.

5. Far behind the leaders, hopelessly beaten, a lone runner gives it everything he has, excited because he is breaking his personal record.

6. One of the best runners in the United States switches events in the TAC meet because his primary goal is to make the U.S. team and compete in Europe.

7. Billy Mills surprises the world with a miraculous homestretch sprint in the Olympic 10,000, and he hits the tape with arms thrown high in triumph.

8. A 39-year-old nuclear physicist jogs across the finish line in 369th place, well-satisfied with himself.

9. Jim Grelle, beaten by all the great milers, continues to improve after his peers quit. At age 28, he becomes fourth fastest of all time, and at age 29 he has run more sub-four-minute miles than anybody.

Obviously, each of these people has a common interest in running, but each one has a different motivation:

Number one runs for the sheer joy of movement. She is like a playful puppy bounding around the yard, or a colt racing across a pasture. This is a purely animal pleasure derived from the kinesthetic feeling of speed, power and natural freedom.

Anyone who is physically fit likes to run. Children compare well with older runners in their natural endurance, and they run incessantly in their play. They gradually lose this pleasure if they don't exercise, but it is regained with renewed interest in sports.

Horace Ashenfelter, who won the 1952 Olympic steeplechase championship at the age of 29, said, "I do enjoy running purely for the sake of the run itself."

Ron Clarke, once the fastest distance runner of all time, said, "I thoroughly enjoy running 100 miles a week. If I didn't, I wouldn't do it."

Man evolved as a running animal. Although slower on two legs than most large animals on four, he needed to run to save his hide and to track down his food; his speed and endurance grew to exceed that of many animals. A child has the natural ability to run down a jack rabbit in an enclosed field where the rabbit cannot hide. And with this ability comes the pleasure of using it. Most sports include running as part of the fun.

All over the world, millions of people run for fun. They run like children, for sheer joy. A little older, their games take on more formality, and they play tag or run impromptu races. When they reach the age of formal games, they run by the hour in basketball, soccer, rugby and less active pursuits. As adults, if they are wise, they continue some sort of activity for their health. They could do many healthy exercises, but most prefer jogging or playing games that include running, such as handball and tennis. The fact is — people like to run.

And this pleasure is the first step for anyone who will later become a competitive runner. Lydiard of New Zealand, one of the world's greatest coaches, said,[77] "Run for fun, and from the fun will come the will to excel."

Number two runs primarily for physical fitness. At age 43 she has come to enjoy jogging, but her original purpose was to gain fitness. A year ago she saw what jogging did for her bridge-club friend, and she could see herself in the mirror. Now her eyes sparkle and her cheeks glow with health. Her figure is slim where nature intended it to be. She is proud of her appearance, and she is proud because her doctor says this exercise will add years of trouble-free enjoyment to her life. Most of all, she rejoices in how much better she feels. She has that euphoric feeling from new energy.

Number three is Jim Ryun, and thousands of other boys who want to be athletes. They want to be athletes because the people they are around the most regard athletes as special people. If our culture praised chess players, perhaps teen-age boys would play more chess, but as it is now they want to be athletes.

Not every boy is big enough and strong enough to be a football player. He may lack the batting eye of a baseball player, and the agility and height of a basketball player. Ryun did. But when he barely made the B team in cross-country, Ryun said, "I thought I was on cloud nine or something. I was very excited about it."[88]

That was how it started with Ryun, and he became as famous throughout the world as any baseball, basketball or football player you can name. All he wanted, at first, was to be some kind of athlete.

Number four, the teacher, remains in competition because he enjoys having friends who have a common respect. Gregariousness is one of our strongest natural drives. We need friends. And we prefer friends who appreciate what we are trying to do — friends with a common interest.

An oddity with runners, if you observe them carefully before, during, and after a big meet, is that they prefer the company of their competitors. You will find strong rivals socializing with each other. The rivalry serves to bolster their respect for each other. If you are devoting your free time to running, you like to be with friends who understand your goals and your sacrifices.

This sentiment was expressed by Bob Deines, one of America's best marathon runners: "Road racing is really something . . . You should see the road races in New England. They are real family social affairs. Everyone who's married brings his family every week. Everyone's relaxed and friendly. That's what I love about it."

Jock Semple, Mr. Marathon, has simple reasons for running: "My doctrine is that the health and friendships derived from running are reward enough."

One of the fastest distance runners of the 1950s, Gordon Pirie of Great Britain, said, "What do I expect to get out of all this? That is simple: enjoyment, physical well-being, self-discipline, a sense of achievement, and world-wide friendships."

Number five runs hard to break his personal record because striving is a natural part of the human inheritance. We evolved as struggling animals who raised ourselves above the rest by trying. It is not only natural for us to work hard, but it brings us pleasure.

Lydiard[77] has said, "It is a simple alloyed joy to tackle yourself on the battlefield of your own physical well-being and come out the victor. There are no war wounds, no scars, only the honors you award yourself for personal physical achievement.''

Psychologists tell us hard work is an important factor in making a man happy. Bertrand Russell said, "Consistent purpose is not enough to make life happy, but it is an almost indispensable condition of a happy life.''

Alfred Adler, the great psychologist, wrote: ". . . we shall always find in human beings . . . this struggle to rise from an inferior to a superior position, from defeat to victory, from below to above. It begins in earliest childhood and continues to the end of our lives . . . The striving for perfection is innate in the sense that it is a part of life, a striving, an urge, a something without which life would be unthinkable.''

Number six has more than one reason for running, but his immediate goal is material success. At first, he won ribbons and medals, but he soon realized their value has only symbolic. Then he began to win watches, radios and tape recorders. These have a real value, but he was soon aware that they could be earned in easier ways.

But a European tour is something of great value. It would cost him $2000 dollars for the trip alone — although he could not buy the invitations a visiting athlete receives. He considers it a valuable prize for someone who would be running anyway.

In actual material benefits, a good athlete has much to gain. Bob Mathias gained a movie career and a place in Congress. Jesse Owens received fabulous offers after his Berlin triumphs. Athletes are offered good jobs because of their names, after athletic scholarships have paid for their college educations. In the 1980s, under the new rules, the best runners can remain amateurs and make a good living.

Number seven, Billy Mills, is a shining example of a runner who finally reached the pinnacle of fame and glory after years of less distinguished racing. He knew all along he was better than the results showed, and he wanted to prove it — to himself, and to the world. When he hit the tape at the Tokyo Olympics, he knew he had matched his speed and endurance and brains and courage against the best in the world, and had beaten them convincingly. He earned the right to be proud of himself for the rest of his life.

For Mills, the track world appreciated his accomplishment, but with slower runners a solitary self-approval is enough. Many a runner is proud of his efforts in a losing race. A man's ego is his own thing, and he is the sole judge of what satisfies it.

Number eight runs for more obscure reasons. His rewards are within himself and they have nothing to do with fame and glory, with medals and watches, with records and championships. His reasons for running lie in the mystique of character building.

One articulate road runner, Joe Henderson, calls it, ". . . A highly personal struggle with forces that can be more ruthless than any human competition." Bob McMillen, who almost won the 1952 Olympic 1500 meters, said he ran for ". . . the inner satisfaction of proving himself capable and strong enough to face the trials of competition and the training program."

Thre are two kinds of people in the world — those who drift and those who try. The drifters believe they are victims of fate, of their inherited tendencies, of the actions of their parents. They believe society shapes people and controls them, and they blame all their troubles on someone else.

The ones who try believe people shape society. They believe in trying to control their lives, to make changes, to improve themselves. It is as if they are waging a personal war on the degenerative forces of a society bent on comfort at the expense of health, self-discipline and self-reliance.

There is no stronger character-builder than self-imposed discipline common to that of a distance runner. This psychological stress, applied gradually, produces an increased acceptance of self-discipline. As a result, you will willingly do what is right, for yourself and society, and you will take pride in your ability. For example, track athletes get better grades in school than the average athlete and far better than the average non-athlete.

Number nine is a combination of all these motives for running. He believes in the individual mystique of self-reliance, and he tries as hard as any runner. He enjoys running and feeling fit. He values the friends he makes in the track world. He likes to win, but he does not quit because he cannot win every race. Many runners enjoy training more than racing. For some, it is a way of life.

Ron Clarke said, "I still cannot define precisely my joy in running. There is no sacrifice in it. I lead what I regard as a normal life."

Roscoe Lee Browne, former indoor AAU champion and now a television actor, had many reasons for running: "Competing is a performance . . . a narcissistic delight." He said, "Track offers perhaps the most wonderful camaraderie," and "When in condition I feel euphoric."

Men race each other on foot for many reasons, but somewhere in their motivation is in-bred desire to compete on a basic level, for no other sport has such world-wide appeal. If you run a distance for time, you can compare yourself with more people than in any other sport in the world.

The answer, then, to the question, "Who should run?": Everybody.

"Who should *race*?" is another question.

Not everyone is suited to compete in distance races. Some people are too young or too old. Some have physical handicaps. Some are too big. Some lack natural endurance. A few lack the necessary speed and agility.

But it is impossible to be too short. Many great distance runners are about 5 feet 6 inches. In general, as the length of the race shortens, the competitors become taller. Among good 10,000-meter runners, Emil Zatopek was 5 feet 8½ inches; Naftali Temu, 5 feet 6 inches, and Max Truex, 5 feet 5½ inches, but Gordon Pirie was 6 feet 2 inches, and AAU champion Jack Bacheler was an exceptional 6 feet 6 5/8 inches. Sergei Popov, 1958 European marathon champion of Russia, was only 5 feet 3½ inches.

Your height makes little difference, but you should be lightly built to be competitive. Bacheler weighed only 164 pounds. Truex weighed 128. Ron Clarke may be the heaviest runner at 5 feet 11 inches and 168 pounds.

Your mental attitude has far more to do with your running success. A lazy man will never make it.

The best way to find out about your natural talent is to do some running. Start by jogging. Increase as you feel like it. After a few months, compare yourself with members of the cross-country or track team. If you seem to have better-than-average ability, give some thought to racing.

What running you do will not be wasted. It will condition you for other sports. If you decide to continue, your first step is to understand how to train.

2

Stress: How Your body Adapts

There are many different ways to train for distance running, and some are better than others. Before you begin to train, you should understand *why* you are training in a certain way. Thus, it is important that you study the various principles of training and how stress relates.

The word "stress" has many meanings. It is used here as Dr. Hans Selye[122] uses it ". . . a stimulus which taxes, strains, or lays a burden upon your body." You suffer stress if you are too cold or too hot, if you are emotionally upset, if you are afraid, hungry or tired. Whatever the stress, your body reacts to it. The way your body reacts is your first lesson in how to train, for training is nothing more than a deliberate stress (or stimulus) in order to gain a specific reaction (or response).

When you train, you do something over and over again so you can do it with greater ease the next time. Celeste Ulrich[134] explains it this way: "Whenever the homeostatic balance of the body is upset, the human organism attempts to adjust in such a way that the balance is restored. Until the balance is restored, a state of stress exists." Thus, if you run enough, your body will adjust to the stress of running and you will be in better condition. That is training.

The science and art of training lies in deciding how far to run, and how fast. Before you can make that decision you need some information. You need to know how your body reacts to various stresses, and particularly to the stress of running.

Your first lesson is on Dr. Selye's General Adaptation Syndrome. He says your body reacts to stress in three stages:

1) The Alarm Reaction

This is divided into two reactions: shock and countershock.

Shock. Your first reaction to stress is shock. A very severe stress causes your heart to pump furiously; your blood pressure falls, your

19

muscles lose tone and feel weak, and small ulcers appear in your stomach and intestines. A very weak stress, such as jogging to warm up, causes only a faster heart beat and a few changes in your blood.

Countershock. Almost immediately after the shock reaction, your body prepares to fight back: Your pituitary gland, at the base of your brain, sounds the alarm by sending out the hormones ACTH and STH as messengers. These messengers speed along your bloodstream at more than nine inches per second until they reach your adrenal glands, above your kidneys. The outside border of an adrenal gland is called the cortex. When the messengers from your pituitary gland arrive, the cortex in turn sends out other hormone messengers, including cortisone.

These messengers rush out and start an amazing series of reactions in your body. Most immediate are increased concentrations of glycogen in your liver and sugar in your blood for use as your muscles need it. Your blood pressure rises. Your whole body metabolism is stimulated. Many important changes are made as your body mobilizes its resources to meet the challenge.

2) The Stage of Resistance

If the stress continues, or if it is repeated over and over again, as in training, your body goes into this second stage. It repairs all your damages and overcompensates by building up your resistance to that particular stress so that the same stress cannot harm you again.

Fred Wilt[140] has an apt comparison for your body's remarkable ability to change: "Vaccinate a man for smallpox with a small dose of appropriate strength vaccine. The body adapts itself to this small infection, and overcompensates by producing antibodies of sufficient quantity to ward off and withstand exposure to the disease at a future date. Break an arm, set it properly, and nature overcompensates by healing the break so thoroughly that it is relatively impossible to break the same spot again. Vaccinate the runner with a small dose of running . . . the body adapts to this low-grade stress, and overcompensates in the resistance it produces to this intensity of training."

Running, of the proper kind, causes many beneficial changes in your body. These will be discussed later. For now, it is enough to know that proper training consists of stressing the body enough to cause these improvements.

If the stress is not too severe, and if you furnish your body with enough of the proper raw materials in the form of nutrition, this progressive adaptation can continue indefinitely.

3) The State of Exhaustion

This does not mean merely that you become exhausted after a hard run. In Selye's State of Exhaustion, your body's adaptation mechanism becomes overloaded and collapses.

Edward G. Jacoby commented on this: "Secondary considerations show, in the studies of adrenal functioning, that those experimental animals which were in the high-intensity program (70 percent or above) reacted to this stress for a period of time, then began to retrogress, showing symptoms of fatigue. Concerning the dropping off in performance, it was demonstrated that overstimulation of the suprarenal gland caused a depletion of adaptation hormones and consequently the ability to adapt to stress was lost.[33]

When that happens you are in trouble. You can no longer train hard without seriously damaging your body. Severe stress can result in prolonged shock and death.

Forbes Carlile, Australian swimming coach and former marathon runner, tells a story about two world-record-holding swimmers at the 1952 Olympics: "Their times started to fall off. One swimmer believed he should train harder, for, as he said, 'Did not slower speed show the need for more training?' The other swimmer eased off and swam slowly when he trained. He spent most of his time in bed. The wrongly advised, energetic one, by a long way failed to come up to his previous standard, but the 'lazy' one, who had developed a sound philosophy on the subject of training, won his Olympic race in record time. Their story well illustrates an application of the General Adaptation Syndrome."[17]

That seems simple enough. You train hard until you reach the stage of failing adaptation, then rest. And, in fact, that tells us the basic science of training, except for one point. You should ease off *before* your adaptation mechanism begins to fail. The difficulty lies in knowing when you are approaching the limit. Here are some warnings:

Mental symptoms of staleness. You feel chronically tired. You lose enthusiasm for training and competing. You become more irritable, even bad tempered. You lose your appetite. You feel listless, lack concentration, and need unusual effort to continue trying.

Physical symptoms of staleness. You feel aches and pains, usually in your joints and muscles. You have trouble relaxing and sleeping. You may have intestinal upsets or a blocked nose and one-day colds. You may notice that you sigh frequently, your outstretched hand trembles, or you look pale. You may have hives or swollen lymph glands, especially in your groin. You are more apt to be injured.

Physical symptoms you can check yourself. You lose weight. Your resting pulse rate rises. Your performances become worse in training and in races.

More obscure physical symptoms. Lower blood pressure, a lower red corpuscle count and decreased hemoglobin values. Experienced sportsmedicine experts can detect overtraining with the electrocardiograph or heartometer.

Any of these symptoms may appear whether you are a beginner or a veteran runner. Anyone can train too hard. On the other hand, the longer you have trained while progressively adapting to more and more stress, the harder you can run without reaching the stage of failing adaptation.

Thus, perfect training must be conducted according to these basic rules:

1) You must train hard enough to put a stress on your body so that it will adapt to even harder running.

2) You must progress gradually so as to avoid reaching the stage of failing adaptation.

3) You must train various parts of your body so that every useful part adapts to its maximum, for anything less than maximum adaptation in any area means you have not reached your full potential.

In the next few chapters we will discuss your various training goals and how to train for the maximum in each.

3

How to Train for Aerobic Endurance

You can improve your speed only about 10 percent. You can improve your strength about 300 percent, but most of it has no value for distance running. You can improve your endurance 2000 percent or more, and all of it is useful.

If you want to know how to gain maximum endurance, it may help if you understand some of the physiology involved. There are many determinant factors in your total endurance, including your mental and emotional control, your speed, strength, and skill, and your anaerobic (without oxygen) muscle endurance. But the majority of your increased endurance — probably 80 or 90 percent — will come from your improvement in supplying fuel and oxygen to your muscles.

The fuel comes from carbon and hydrogen (carbohydrates) in the food you eat, and the oxygen comes from the air you breathe. The way your muscle cells receive and use oxygen and fuel is one of the marvels of the human body. You can improve this capacity to use fuel and oxygen in many ways.

HOW TO SEND MORE OXYGEN TO YOUR BLOOD

When you expand your chest cavity, air rushes into your lungs. This fresh air is almost 21 percent oxygen, but after mixing with "used" air in your lungs, it reaches your alveoli with only about 14.5 percent oxygen.

You have about 750 million alveoli. These tiny sacs allow the air to touch a very thin double membrane over an amazing total surface the size of a small city block. On the other side of this membrane is your blood in pulmonary capillaries. Because the pressure of the oxygen in your alveoli is about two and a half times as great as the

23

pressure of the oxygen in this venous blood, oxygen molecules diffuse (dissolve) through the membrane and into your red blood cells.

Your lungs improve their capacity to send fresh oxygen to your blood. This involves several changes: Your diaphragm becomes larger and stronger, and your respiratory muscles become stronger and more flexible so that your chest cavity can expand and contract more. This allows more air to enter your lungs. Your alveolar tissue grows larger and you actually grow more alveoli, and it becomes easier for oxygen to diffuse into your blood.

Physiologists have proved that a runner inhales six times more oxygen than his blood can transport. Although this is undoubtedly true from a technical viewpoint, it is small consolation to you when you are gasping for breath. This extra breathing is believed necessary to remove waste products. And physiologists agree that it is possible to exercise hard enough so that your blood, rushing through your lungs 10 times each minute in its hurry to deliver oxygen to your muscles, leaves your lungs with less than a full load of oxygen. If you believe in trying everything that might help you improve, you'll try to improve your breathing.

Many coaches and runners believe you do not need to make any effort to breathe properly, since the amount of air you breathe is regulated automatically by the needs of your body. It is the complicated result of oxygen, carbon dioxide, the acid content of your blood and your neural mechanisms.

But there are three indications that you need better respiration than you develop naturally with training:

• Athletes expand their maximum ventilation by more than 50 percent; this would not happen unless they needed more air for running.

• Physiologists report that you can reach your maximum aerobic capacity without reaching your maximum breathing capacity. Beyond your aerobic capacity, when you run hard enough to use your anaerobic mechanism, your breathing increases much more. In the final stages of exhaustion, you gasp for air. This indicates you are not breathing as much as your body desires.

• And physiologists have discovered an "artificial deficit." As your cardiac output increases with harder running, the amount of oxygen carried in your hemoglobin tends to decrease.[7] This means your blood does not pick up as much oxygen in your lungs as it is capable of carrying. Each gram of hemoglobin slips from its natural carrying capacity of 1.34 milliliters of oxygen to a level as low as

1.24 milliliters. At the same time, your hemoglobin value rises, compensating to some extent. But many top athletes show a decrease in the amount of oxygen they can carry in their arteries during increased exercise. Asmussen says, "The main reason is, no doubt, that the diffusion becomes incomplete."[3]

If this is true — if your arteries carry less oxygen than they should because of inefficient collection from your lungs — then you certainly should consider trying to breathe more efficiently. You should do it on the basis of the shotgun theory, hoping that something might help. You should try it because of the "last inch" theory (which states that it takes only an imperceptible improvement to give you that last inch you need for victory). And you might be inclined to try it because the U.S. Olympic coaches in 1968 thought enough of respiration to allow a coach to work with the runners' breathing.

If you want to make the effort, you should begin by learning to distinguish between chest breathing and diaphragm breathing. Your conscious thought when you want to breathe deeply is to lift and expand your chest, but it is possible to breathe with very little chest movement. Your diaphragm, a dome-shaped muscle separating your chest cavity from your abdomen, expands and contracts, enlarging your chest cavity to allow more air to enter.

You can test it easily. Force out all the air you can by depressing your chest and ribs. You can now force out a little more with your diaphragm, and you can breathe in and out without changing the position of your chest and ribs. Professional singers and speakers develop strength and flexibility in their diaphragms. If a runner can do it, he can increase his total breathing capacity with less oxygen-supported effort.

In anaerobic running, however, diaphragm breathing is not enough. Your chest muscles must be developed and your ribs must become more flexible. Much of this will come about through hard running, but you may help it develop by consciously expanding and contracting your chest walls to their maximum several times a day.

Anaerobic running requires deeper breathing because of your increased need to eliminate wastes. Therefore, *exhaling* is more important than inhaling. Inhaling must naturally follow exhaling, but full and complete exhaling does not come about naturally. You must practice.

Even if you do not want to improve your running, you should learn to breathe properly. Most people breathe up to 20 times a minute at rest and they inhale only about one-eighth of their maximum possible amount of air. Since a large part of your vital capacity is "dead space" (where blood cannot reach the oxygen), this means you are mixing very little fresh oxygen with your stale alveolar air. In order to prevent pockets where your alveolar air "stagnates," you should exhale more air with each breath.

Captain William F. Knowles of London, who has been consulted by more than 60,000 sufferers from respiratory complaints, said, "Real breath control means learning to control the way we *exhale,* not the way we *inhale . . .* The more air we exhale, the more we can breathe in." As an additional bonus, he points out that "careful breath control, with emphasis on exhaling, helps us to relax under any kind of tension or stress."

Forced exhaling makes room for more oxygen in the far reaches of your alveoli. But if you force more air out, more must enter. Therefore, when you breathe more deeply, you must breathe more slowly. One woman trained herself to the point where her normal breathing is only four breaths per minute.

One recommended method of breathing is in rhythm with your strides. For borderline running, one forced exhale can be followed by inhaling naturally for three counts. As you run faster, you must inhale for only two counts. The secret is the rapid exhale.

Dr. George Sheehan, himself a marathoner, wrote, "Belly-breathing plus exhaling against resistance is the answer to the stitch. It is also the formula for correct breathing."[123]

Experiment to find your way. But be sure to breathe deeply enough so that you never get so far behind that your regulatory system has to speed up your breathing.

Physiologists in Bulgaria learned in 1953 that consciously regulated breathing (including full exhaling with each breath) makes a remarkable difference in oxygen intake and carbon dioxide separation.[69] In easy exercise, oxygen intake was increased 17 percent and carbon dioxide separation was increased 40 percent.

The most important single effort you should make is to form the habit of exhaling more air at the end of each breath by thrusting a little harder with your diaphragm. To be certain you are not limiting yourself by poor ventilation, do this:

• Develop the strength of your breathing muscles by hard running and harder deep breathing.

• Form the habit of exhaling with long and slow breaths, both at rest and running.

• Practice consciously while doing easy running so as to form a habit you can use during hard running.

YOUR BLOOD CAN CARRY MORE OXYGEN

About 7.7 percent of your body weight is blood. About 55 percent of your blood is plasma (91 percent water). The other 45 percent of your blood is cells, mostly red cells (erythrocytes or red corpuscles).

The most critical job your blood must perform is to carry oxygen to your tissues. But the aforementioned composition of blood could not carry enough oxygen in saturation to provide for your needs. Nature found a remarkable way to increase this carrying capacity 50 times — by adding hemoglobin to your red blood cells. About 95 percent of the dry weight of red cells is hemoglobin.

Heme is a metal complex containing iron. Globin is a colorless protein. Hemoglobin contains about 65 percent of all the iron in your body. This purple hemoglobin combines with oxygen to form oxyhemoglobin, a scarlet-red compound. Fully saturated, your blood can thus carry oxygen amounting to about 20 percent of its volume, a truly remarkable feat of logistics.

Kalevi Rompotti, the Finnish coach, said, "It is clear that the more hemoglobin, i.e. iron, the red corpuscles contain (the redder the blood is) the more oxygen it will be able to carry from the lungs to the muscles. The more there are of these red corpuscles, i.e. the more blood the runner possesses, the larger the hemoglobin surface which is available to combine with oxygen in the lungs and to deliver oxygen to the muscles. From the standpoint of endurance, it is therefore of primary importance to the runner that he possess as much blood as possible with as much iron in his blood as possible."[108]

The average number of red blood cells is 4.5 million to 5.5 million per cubic millimeter. Normal hemoglobin content is somewhere between 14 and 16 grams per 100 cubic centimeters of blood. A Finnish skier was measured at 6.5 million and 18 grams. Some 1960 Olympic athletes had similar values. Another group of Olympic athletes averaged 16 grams of hemoglobin, ranging from 13.7 to 18.6.

Some simple arithmetic will convince you of the amazing possibilities for improvement in your running if you can raise your red cell and hemoglobin values. (These values parallel each other, so for all practical purposes an improvement in one is an improvement in the other.)

If your heart can pump 30 liters of blood per minute and you have a hemoglobin value of 14.5, you will send about 5.78 liters of oxygen to your capillaries each minute. (If 90 percent of that oxygen is used and you weigh 154 pounds, your oxygen uptake would be 74.3 milliliters per kilogram of body weight, making you a potentially fair distance runner.) Then suppose you increased your hemoglobin to 18.0 without changing any other activity. This means 7.18 liters of oxygen would reach your capillaries each minute, and your oxygen capacity would shoot up to 92.3. You could be a super runner, and break all world records.

Apparently, such an incredible improvement is not possible. One reason may be that an overcrowded bloodstream cannot add that much more oxygen. (Normally, each gram of hemoglobin picks up about 1.34 milliliters of oxygen, but a careful measurement showed some top athletes carry as little as 1.24 milliliters.) Some physiologists have proved that when your blood becomes thicker with red blood cells, your heart automatically pumps less blood. Such an adjustment happens during easy exercise or rest. During maximum exercise, *some* benefit is obtained from having a high percentage of oxygen in your blood — either your aerobic capacity improves or your heart pumps more easily and efficiently.

Physiologists list many possibilities for this lack of efficiency in saturating your blood with oxygen during hard running. A slight "arterial deficit" has been noted during rest, when the maximum amount of oxygen saturation is not reached. This deficit increases about five-fold during exercise. Possible answers include use of some of the oxygen by your hard-working heart, a poor mix of oxygen in the far reaches of your lungs, or from "the mixed venous blood bypassing the alveoli in direct shunts to the arteries."[3]

But whatever the reason for this inefficiency, the more efficient you can make it — the more oxygen you carry in your blood — the better you will run. Any increase in your red blood cell count or in your hemoglobin value increases your capacity to carry oxygen.

You produce more red cells in the marrow of your bones whenever you need them, if the necessary raw materials are present in your body.[145] Since the average life of a red cell is only 120 days and, in addition, many are destroyed during exercise, you need this ability to produce new cells. The capacity of your bone marrow to produce new cells can increase six to eight times.[145]

Until your bone marrow produces enough red cells to meet your oxygen-carrying needs, you may be said to suffer from anemia. Anemia means "without blood." When you have anemia, too little oxygen reaches your tissues to produce normal energy. Anemia is a result of a low red cell count or low hemoglobin value, or both. Anemia is caused by one of three things:

- Bleeding, or donation of blood.
- Faulty production of new cells in your bone marrow.
- Destruction of red blood cells in your body.

Red blood cells are destroyed in several ways, but a healthy athlete is concerned only with destruction by exercise. The life of a red blood cell is hazardous: "Each cell travels through the circulation in 45 seconds . . . The physical wear and tear of the long journey involves compression and decompression as well as swelling and shrinking during exchange of oxygen and carbon dioxide and of ions . . . Eventually, the red cell becomes mechanically fragile or chemically defective and is destroyed in the small vessels of the body . . . Rous (1933) found the cells threshed to bits, fragmented and dissociated by circulation stresses."[70]

Some physiologists say the violent contraction of your muscles in running crushes some red cells. Davidson proved that many red cells are destroyed in your feet, especially while running on hard surfaces.[53]

Many physiologists' studies have found that severe or prolonged exercise decreases red cell count and hemoglobin values. Farris stated: "The total number of erythrocytes per cubic millimeter increased in the short-time athletic events, but decreasd in events which required over 25 minutes."[44] This includes most modern training sessions.

Orias, a French physiologist, "concluded that there was a real drop in hemoglobin in his subjects after 15 days of intense exercise."[127] This lowering of hemoglobin value all out of proportion to a drop in red cell count was explained by the fact that newly formed red cells do not yet have their full content of hemoglobin.[83]

Four days of hard exercise by dogs reduced their red cell count by 19 percent. Strenuous marches caused many men to show traces of hemoglobin and hematin in their blood serum and urine — evidence of injury to the blood. Long and strenuous mountain climbing reduced the red count and percent of hemoglobin.[16]

Symptoms a runner might experience after rapid destruction of blood include sudden weakness, indefinite discomfort, headache, restlessness, irritability, pain in the back, legs, and arms, loss of appetite and weight, pallor, jaundice, dark stools, red urine, nausea, vomitting, diarrhea, abdominal pain, shaking chills and fever.[145]

And, of course, there is the symptom of slower running performances. Dr. Peter Karpovich reports cases of runners who donated a pint of blood and immediately lost their ability to run well.[64]

From the facts just mentioned you can see that improvement in the capacity of your blood to carry oxygen involves both positive and negative factors. You must do what you can to increase your red cells and hemoglobin value while at the same time you try to avoid their destruction. You can make use of four methods:

• A shortage of oxygen causes your bone marrow to produce more red cells. Therefore, if you stay at a high altitude long enough, your blood values will increase. David Dill[32] reported that 10 men in his party averaged hemoglobin values of 18.4 after several weeks at altitudes between 10,000 and 17,500 feet. This is far above the average value of around 15 and even above that of the Olympic athletes. Dill tested 10 men who had lived at 17,500 feet for two to 14 years and found amazing hemoglobin values ranging from 18.4 to 25.5 gram/100 milliliters. Dill concluded, "Increased blood volume and red cell volume undoubtedly play a major role in exercise at high altitude, but may not be of much advantage at sea level."[32]

Other physiologists report that an increased red cell count increases its viscosity and therefore decreases its flow through your blood vessels. Others report improved performances at sea level after acclimatization at altitude. Perhaps the most dramatic result was that of Lon Spurrier in 1955.

Spurrier, a relatively unknown half-miler, spent about two weeks at Mexico City's 7300-foot altitude before the Pan American Games. Two days after his return to sea level, well-rested, he shocked the track world with a 1:47.5 880, 1.1 seconds under the world record and 2.3 seconds faster than he had ever run before.

• Training of the proper kind increases your blood volume, red cell count, and hemoglobin value. Some physiologists report that an average man can increase the amount of blood in his body by as much as one-and-a-half quarts (33 percent). Torgny Sjostrand[126] reported an average of 74 milliliters of blood per kilogram of body weight, with wrestlers and weightlifters having 73, cyclists 79, and runners 88.

Changes in your blood are so frequent and so rapid that learning the exact situation at all times is impossible without frequent blood tests. Usually, when you begin training after a layoff, your red cell count drops, not only because of destruction of the cells but because your blood plasma increases in volume and dilutes your blood. For that reason, you can expect your red cell count and your hemoglobin value to drop during the first weeks of training. After a few months, production will catch up with demand and you will have more red cells and more hemoglobin than before — unless you train too hard.

The question of how to train in order to increase your blood values is difficult to answer. Sjostrand observed less increase from moderate exercise of long duration than from short intervals varying up to exhaustion. Another experiment[96] found speed training to increase blood values more than longer runs. This may be true because harder running destroys more blood cells and thus stimulates your bone marrow to produce new cells faster.

On the other hand, longer workouts would also create a need for oxygen, which in turn stimulates production. Therefore, with the information now known, it would seem that no particular training should be adopted solely to increase blood values. A proper mixture of running will probably give your bone marrow all the stimulation it needs.

You cannot produce new red blood cells and hemoglobin if you do not furnish your body with the proper building materials. To build the heme of your hemoglobin you need iron in your diet. To build globin you need protein. Fortunately, iron is so plentiful you need not worry about a shortage, unless you live on refined foods, or are female.

You need from 12 to 15 milligrams of iron daily, more while you are forming myoglobin and hemoglobin as you train. Here are a few foods high in iron:

eggs	1.1 mg
lean beef	1 mg per ounce
medium-sized chicken liver	2.5 mg
kidney	3.8 mg per ounce
calf liver	4 mg per ounce
pork liver	8 mg per ounce
clams	1.8 mg per ounce
lettuce	2 mg per one-fourth head
soybeans	5.4 mg per cup
canned or dried apricots	8 mg per cup
dried dates	5.7 mg per cup
canned prune juice	9.8 mg per cup
whole wheat bread	0.5 mg per slice
brown rice	4 mg per cup
nuts	about 3 mg per one-half cup
dessicated liver	6 mg per one-fourth cup
torula yeast	7 mg per one-fourth cup

Thus, lack of iron is seldom the important factor in anemia. Vitamin B_6 deficiency anemia, for example, not only cannot be corrected by giving iron, but iron can damage tissues.[51] However, 100 milliliters of vitamin B_6 daily has produced a rapid increase of hemoglobin value from 8.5 to 13.

Anemia has been produced by withholding magnesium from men's diets.[124] Lack of folic acid can result in anemia; your bone marrow will start producing red cells soon after folic acid is taken.[49]

Anemia has also been connected with lack of vitamins B$_1$, B$_2$, niacin, pantothenic acid, cholin,[135] and with copper, cobalt and proteins.[121]

Probably the anemia of most concern to runners is caused by a deficiency of vitamin E, which also helps decrease your body's need for oxygen.[148] This anemia has been produced by depriving men of vitamin E.[54] This lack of the vitamin not only hinders iron absorption and formation of hemoglobin, but it causes red cells to be destroyed more rapidly.[54] Biopsies showed that 280 milliliters of vitamin E daily for five days cleared up bone marrow abnormalities, and the anemia was corrected.[67]

Vitamin C decreases your need for vitamin E and helps avoid anemia,[31] but no iron can help if you lack vitamin E. This vitamin is probably the hardest to find in our foods and could well be the most advisable supplement to add to your food.

If you eat a well-balanced diet of unrefined foods and include liver frequently, you will give your body all the building materials it needs to keep up the quality of your blood, with the possible exception of vitamin E.

One other method of aiding your bone marrow to increase your blood values is rest. It has been well established by physiologists that after severe exercise has destroyed red blood cells, a few days of rest will restore those values. Practical experience has proved that rest is necessary before an optimum endurance run or after severe training. Lately, much of the credit has gone to Selye's adaptation to stress, but more blood tests will undoubtedly confirm that some of the credit must go to increased oxygen carrying capacity of the blood.

An English distance runner who had been training and racing hard went into a slump, and also complained of several ailments. His blood count showed a hemoglobin value of 14.8. He stopped racing, reduced his training, and in four weeks he had regained his form. His blood count showed a hemoglobin value of 16.5, the day *after* a good race.

The importance of proper rest, especially before a major race, cannot be emphasized too strongly. Roger Bannister's five days of rest before the first sub-four-minute mile, and Don Bowden's four days before he ran the first sub-four-minute mile by an American are well known. Neither could have done it without the time away from training. Other reserves fill up, too, with rest, but your blood values make the most dramatic improvement.

Nobody can prove how important blood is unless blood tests are given at the proper time. Kalevi Rompotti said, "I consider it absolutely necessary that blood tests be given athletes preparing for important competition for a period of at least six months, and a minimum of once per month during this half year."[108]

The importance of the oxygen-carrying capacity of your blood has been sensationalized in recent years by scientific experiments and rumors about so-called blood doping.

Blood Doping

The use of this term was unfortunate because it implied the use of drugs, even though none were used. A better term for the process of increasing the hemoglobin content of the blood is "blood boosting."

The original experiment was performed in Sweden by Bjorn Ekblom.[41] He withdrew 800 milliliters of blood from three subjects. Their hemoglobin concentration decreased 13 percent and work capacity fell 30 percent. After 14 days, hemoglobin had returned to normal. After four weeks, each subject's blood was reinfused into him and he was tested again. Hemoglobin increased 13 percent in one day and work capacity increased 23 percent!

Immediately, coaches and runners became excited at the possibilities. Rumors ran wild, especially centering on the most successful distance runner of recent years, Lasse Viren. But no use of blood boosting has been admitted or proved.

There are several possible reasons why blood boosting may not improve performances:

• Ekblom's tests were not made on trained athletes, and the increase in work capacity could have been psychological.

• Many tests have proved you cannot increase your work capacity arithmetically in relation to an increase in hemoglobin. Your blood apparently carries a limited amount of oxygen. Increasing the density of oxygen is balanced by a decrease in the amount of blood pumped. Part of the reason may be the fact that a larger red blood cell count means an increase in your blood's viscosity. Thick blood will not flow as fast.

• If increased hemoglobin resulted in significantly faster times, all altitude training would do the same. No consistent improvements have resulted from the greatly increased amount of altitude training done since the 1968 Olympics.

• If such an easy solution were practical, Soviet and East German runners would break all distance records. No such explosion has happened.

• The few runners who have performed well, and thus came under the cloud of rumors (Vaatainen, Viren, Vasala, Cierpinski, Baumgartl), could have run well because of talent and training methods. No miracles have occurred.

In addition to the possibility of being ineffective, blood boosting may have harmful side effects. Dr. Roger Bannister called it "immoral" and "dangerous." Some doctors have suggested the thick blood could lead to congestive heart failure.

HOW TO INCREASE YOUR CARDIAC OUTPUT

After your blood is saturated with oxygen in the lungs, it flows back to the heart. It enters the upper left chamber (left auricle) of your heart. When the valve opens, the blood drops down into your thick, strong left ventricle. A powerful contraction pumps it into your aorta and then into smaller arteries. It is on its way to your muscles.

Much of your success as a distance runner depends upon how much blood your heart can pump. Your heart grows larger and stronger with use. It enlarges because, like any other muscle, its fibers grow stronger and larger with more use. It also grows larger by dilation or stretching. A larger, trained heart can pump twice as much blood. The size of an average man's heart is about 800 cubic centimeters. Endurance athletes have hearts ranging from 850 to 1460 cubic centimeters.

Your maximum pulse rate will not increase with training. In fact, it may slow by about 5 percent. Therefore, you need another method of pumping more blood.

Stroke Volume

This is done by increasing your stroke volume. Each time your heart beats, it pumps out a certain amount of blood, depending upon your activity and the size and strength of your heart. When you exercise hard enough, your pulse rate and your stroke volume combine to reach a maximum cardiac output. (Cardiac output equals your pulse rate multiplied by your stroke volume.)

An average man may have a maximum cardiac output of 20 liters per minute. If his pulse goes no higher than 200, that means his maximum stroke volume is 100 milliliters for each beat of his heart. A stroke volume of 212 milliliters has been measured in a champion cyclist. (He had a pulse rate of 188, giving him a cardiac output of 39.8 liters per minute.[39])

Thus, if you want to be a distance runner, one of the most important changes you must make in your body is to enlarge your heart and strengthen its pumping capacity. It is the most important part of your system for delivering oxygen to your muscles. The more blood you can pump into your arteries, the more endurance you'll have.

Almost any kind of sustained exercise helps strengthen your heart. Sprinting is not sustained exercise, and so it does little to develop the pumping capacity of your heart. Hours of easy work in which your heart beats a bit faster than at rest will develop your cardiac output somewhat, but not enough to help your distance running significantly.

Almost any training will increase your cardiac output over the years. That is why distance runners usually improve until their late twenties even without ideal training methods.

Controversy has left most runners and coaches in doubt as to the best way to increase cardiac output. The most definite statement on the subject was made in 1958 by the German team including Woldemar Gerschler (a professor of physical education and the famous coach of Rudolph Harbig and Josey Barthel) and Dr. Herbert Reindell (a cardiologist).

After extensive testing, Gerschler and Reindell stated[106] that the greatest stroke volume occurs during the beginning of the rest pause immediately after exercise that has raised your pulse rate to about 180 beats per minute. (A faster pulse results in inefficiency, and so harder running and sprinting cannot produce the desired increase in heart strength.)

Thus, Gerschler's runners train on short interval runs of about 30 seconds, which raise their pulse rates to 180. Then they jog until their pulses drop to about 120, but no longer than a minute and a half. Gerschler claims this method has increased heart size significantly in a few weeks.

Gerschler and Reindell came to this conclusion when their tests showed an increase in oxygen uptake during the rest period. Since nothing else showed a change, they concluded that only an increased stroke volume could account for this phenomenon. They said this was a dilation of the heart, caused by blood rushing into the suddenly relaxed heart. This "expansion stimulus" was said to stretch the size of the heart's cavities, allowing more blood to enter.

Toni Nett concluded in his summary of this theory: "So it is the pause which is of the greatest importance to the adaptation of the circulatory system to endurance performance. The single repeat runs are only preparatory conditions for the stimulus value of the pauses."[94]

For several years, runners used some sort of interval training without further examination of its results. But gradually, certain facts have come to light to counter the Gerschler method:

• Big-name physiologists, particularly Christensen, disputed the theory on the basis of incorrect methodology. They show, contrary to Reindell, that your oxygen uptake does *not* increase when exercise stops. Roskamm Reindell et al obtained their misleading results because they tested subjects who were lying down. This position makes for a stroke volume at least 40 percent higher. When you are standing, the blood cannot rush back to your heart as fast.

• Other possible misconceptions occur: 1) Since your oxygen uptake lags at the start of exercise, your average might not be as high as at the very beginning of your rest pause. 2) Another factor besides stroke volume could cause a higher oxygen uptake: When your muscles suddenly stop contracting, the flow of blood through your capillaries increases.

• The Reindell theory would seem to increase dilation only. You also want a stronger muscular contraction of your heart.

• It is worthy of note that Gerschler is most famous for coaching middle-distance runners. His system has not been outstanding for producing 5000-meter runners, nor distance runners. This indicates that his method does not produce the maximum oxygen uptake.

• In later years, Reindell admitted the possibility of danger to the heart from too much interval work. Toni Nett, long-time spokesman for the theory, wrote in 1964: ". . . now we have to admit that our enthusiasm was exaggerated and the results did not match our expectations. . . There is no better method than interval training to enlarge the heart in the shortest possible time, but, this has its misgivings too — 'easy come, easy go.' The effect is not as stable as the enlarging process of the heart by means of time-consuming long-distance running. There is no doubt in certain cases, (to overcome accidental loss of training time, before big meets or championships) a quick method to enlarge the heart (raising of endurance level) is needed. Nevertheless, this is not without danger to the heart itself, if the repetitions are not planned carefully. . . The short-distance interval training is generally on the way out, although the long-distance interval training continues to thrive as a method of developing general endurance."[95]

Exercise For a Stronger Heart

Now you want to know what kind of exercise *does* develop the strongest heart. One way to study the question is to learn which athletes have the largest and strongest hearts. First, it would be well to admit that the best endurance athletes probably had stronger hearts to begin with. For example, Armin Hary, the Olympic 100-meter champion in 1960, had a heart volume of only 620 cubic centimeters in 1957. With two and one-half years of interval training he increased its size to 860 cubic centimeters, a remarkable development but far short of the 1100 to 1460 cubic centimeters in great endurance athletes.

Tests of German national teams in 1966[112] showed that cyclists had the largest hearts in relation to the size of their bodies. Next came cross-country skiers, boxers, and pentathlon men. Runners were not tested. Weightlifters and gymnasts showed no increase over normal heart volume. These results show a direct relationship between the time you spend in motion and the size of your heart.

When heart size is compared to body size, the figure is given in cubic centimeters per kilogram of body weight. The highest figure in the Roskamm tests was a professional cyclist with 18.9. But Sergei Popov, the 1958 European marathon champion, had a heart volume of 1200 cubic centimeters and he weighed only 118 pounds — a fantastic quotient of 22.4, the largest known.

Only a very small percentage of the best athletes have been measured for heart size or stroke volume, because it is a difficult procedure. In the tests done, cross-country skiers and cyclists show the largest hearts and the strongest stroke volumes. But until physiologists do such measuring of runners, nobody will be absolutely certain who has the largest and strongest hearts, and what it takes to develop them.

In the meantime, a study of what physiologists do know, plus the training methods of runners with exceptional endurance, might reveal part of the secret.

Facts: Although your stroke volume can be increased without increasing your heart size,[114] a larger stroke volume usually, but not always, goes with a larger heart.[40] Larger hearts are found in athletes who exercise for long periods. A shortage of oxygen increases heart size. Dill wrote: "While skeletal muscle doesn't increase in weight at altitude, heart hypertrophy is well documented. Exposing rats to simulated altitudes of 12,000 to 18,000 feet for several weeks increased heart weight by 50 percent without change in the percent of water."[32] This increase in size takes place without extra exercise; the key is the length of time spent with a shortage of oxygen.

Conclusion: Running, at any pace, causes a shortage of oxygen, which will enlarge your heart and thus increase your stroke volume.

Fact: Your heart tends to decrease in size immediately following exercise.[45]

Conclusion: Continuous running means a continuous stimulation. Interval running allows the stimulus to stop.

Facts: Your heart is a muscle. As in a skeletal muscle, the fibers of your heart can shorten or contract on impulse, but they cannot lengthen by themselves. Unlike your skeletal muscles, your heart can relax completely because it has no permanent contraction (tonus). Thus, the amount of blood your ventricle can pump out at each beat depends upon how much is forced in. A trained heart stretches more and allows more blood to enter. It also pumps out a higher percentage of the blood in the ventricle.

Conclusion: In order to increase your stroke volume to the maximum, you must run at a pace that will force the maximum amount of blood into the ventricle.

Facts: Most hearts will beat more than 180 times a minute during severe exercise. This means more than three times each second. A high pulse rate means your ventricles do not have time to wait to be completely filled. Thus, they do not contain as much blood when they contract again, and so your stroke volume decreases.

Conclusion: If you run too fast, you are not improving your stroke volume.

Facts: You can develop strength in your skeletal muscles by weight training. The heavier the weight you move, the fewer times you can move it. But if the weight is so light you can lift it indefinitely, you gain endurance but not maximum strength. A muscle gains maximum strength by the combination of being stressed as much as possible while repeating it enough to stimulate growth.

Conclusion: In strengthening your heart muscle, you must compromise between maximum contractions and sustained effort.

Fact: In three studies, physiologists[5 39 40] tested 44 people. A total of 20 of them did not reach their maximum stroke volumes until they reached their maximum heart rates. Of these 20, however, eight came from the group of 13 highly trained athletes.

Conclusion: Training increases the ability of your heart to maintain a high stroke volume at a high heart rate, but you have no way of knowing, without laboratory tests, how your own heart is reacting.

Facts: Various people recommend various degrees of effort to improve your cardiac output. Dr. M.J. Karvonen[65] found a pulse rate of 153 to be necessary. Reindell[106] found 180 to be necessary (in interval work). Astrand wrote: "You cannot use the heart rate alone to tell how hard an individual should train. If your goal is a heart rate of 180, this will be discouraging for the person with a maximum heart rate of 150! The pulse rate selected should be related to the individual's maximum."[7]

In one suggested formula, your resting heart rate is subtracted from your maximum heart rate. Seventy percent of this is added to your resting rate to give the ideal training pulse. This usually comes out between 140 and 160. Van Aaken[136] advocates a pulse of 130 for general endurance training.

Conclusion: No exact pulse rate is ideal for everybody.

Facts: Taking your heart rate is usually unscientific. The most accurate and meaningful way is to record it electronically while you are running. Otherwise, you must stop running to take your pulse. Your heart rate will slow rapidly after you stop. Thus, if you take it for only five seconds (x 12) you will have a higher pulse rate than if you count it for 15 seconds (x 4). Your pulse will be highest while still walking. Your standing pulse will be higher than sitting. Lying down will give you the lowest pulse rate. Probably the most practical method is to count it for five seconds while standing. Other stimuli, such as strong emotions, also change your heart rate.

Conclusion: Heart rate is unscientific and you should not seriously compare your rate with other runners. But if you count your own in the same way each time, it can be used as a guide.

Fact: Your cardiac output cannot be greater than the flow of blood returning to your heart.

Conclusion: Slow running does not push your cardiac output up to its maximum.

Fact: Since every individual is different, no exact plan can be stated for increasing your stroke volume. Using the conclusions arrived at in the previous statement, it would seem that the greatest improvement would come from the hardest effort you can sustain for a long time.

Conclusion: To increase your stroke volume you should run close to the borderline between your aerobic capacity and your anaerobic oxygen debt. With experience, you can sense this borderline. To be certain you do not run too slowly, you must occasionally venture across the border into oxygen debt. Then you must slow your pace enough to recover.

Fact: The higher you raise your maximum aerobic capacity, the more likely you are to reach your highest stroke volume near your maximum heart rate.[5][39][40]

Conclusion: Your training speed should become progressively faster as your condition improves during the year, and year after year. Borderline running automatically includes this increase in speed.

Fact: If you run slowly, the length of time you can keep it up is not limited by your cardiac output. Other limitations will force you to stop eventually. (This will be considered later.) These same limitations will gradually slow your borderline pace, for to maintain the same pace, you would eventually be forced to cross the border into oxygen debt.

Conclusion: You should not worry about holding the same pace all the way through your borderline run (unless you are training for another purpose).

Facts: Many clues will tell you when you have crossed the border and are building up an oxygen debt. Your breathing becomes hard enough so that conversation is uncomfortable. You begin to feel your heart pound. Your legs feel heavier and may ache in spots. You have more and more difficulty holding your pace.

Conclusion: You should be aware of these symptoms so as to recognize the first one to appear. This will enable you to cross back over the border and continue running for a long time. It is important that you learn to know yourself and be able to separate real fatigue from false symptoms.

Facts: The most important question remaining is: How many miles of borderline running are best for your stroke volume?

Lydiard states flatly that 100 miles a week is best — no more, no less: "The key to my condition training is one hundred miles a week. No runner, training either for the track or the marathon, should run more than that distance. That would cause continual fatigue instead of a steady acceleration of ability. When you can run a hundred miles a week comfortably, the progressive subsequent improvement is not secured by running greater distances, but by aiming to run the same distance a week, faster. . . It must be done at good speeds according to the runner's condition and ability."[77]

The problem may not be quite so simple. Some excellent runners have been successful with fewer miles, and some have trained longer.

Derek Clayton, from 1969 to 1981 the world's fastest marathoner at 2:08:34, was tested on a treadmill by Dr. David Costill. He "could run at better than five minutes per mile without accumulating blood lactic acid."[23] Thus, Clayton's borderline pace would start out around five minutes per mile and slow a little as he used up his supply of glycogen.

John Walker, former world-record holder for the mile, trains with long runs of 10 to 23 miles, usually faster than 6:00 per mile. Amby Burfoot won the Boston Marathon in 1968 after running up to 160 miles a week, but his training speed was not up to his borderline pace. Ron Clarke ran 140 or more miles a week at

Ron Clarke, right, leads Mohamed Gammoudi (781) — the eventual winner Kip Keino and Naftali Temu (575) in the 1968 Olympic Games 5000-meter run. Clarke would finish fifth. The tall, handsome Australian, although he set 21 world records on the track, never won the Olympic gold medal.

borderline pace or faster. Clayton ran about 130 miles at close to borderline.

Dave Bedford trained at 188 miles a week for six weeks (then cut down for two) before his big cross-country victory in 1971. Later, he tried even longer mileage. Gerry Lindgren is supposed to have tried 250 miles a week. It should be noted that Bedford, Lindgren, and others failed after their long-run experiments. There is certainly some limit.

Ernst van Aaken of West Germany advises training longer according to the length of your race — as much as 184 miles a week for marathoners. He suggests walking during long runs rather than quitting once fatigue sets in.

Everybody agrees that you should build up your mileage gradually. They also agree that each individual has unique needs and capabilities.

Conclusion: Although you should think of 100 miles a week as a nice, round number, you should decide according to your own situation and capabilities.

Facts: Any runner is limited in his total mileage by depletion of his glycogen stores. This can result in tight legs, which become sore. You are also limited if your fatigue carries over to the next day.

Conclusion: You should sustain your borderline running only for as long as you can avoid lasting fatigue.

Facts: Cross-country skiers have competed for two and one-half hours with heart rates of 180. One skier completed an 85-kilometer race while his pulse varied from 150 to 180 for almost seven hours.[47]

Conclusion: You should let yourself be limited only by physical restrictions, not by your desire to stop running.

Summary: The farther you stray from the speed of borderline running *in either direction,* the less you stimulate your stroke volume to develop. Run on your borderline for as many miles as you can, comfortably, without carrying over the fatigue to your next workout. If two workouts a day enable you to run more total miles, your stroke volume will improve even more.

You cannot measure your improvement in stroke volume without the complicated laboratory tests. If your running performances improve with less effort, your stroke volume has probably increased, but other improvements may also be involved. Your best proof is a lower pulse rate, both after running and at rest, because that means your heart is pumping more blood with each beat.

Lydiard wrote: "I have known marathon training to bring a runner's pulse rate down from the normal 68 to 45 in three months. All the athletes I train have a pulse rate in the vicinity of 45, with Snell thudding along quietly at an astonishing 38. Their hearts recover this normal slow beat very quickly after exertion."[77]

One other possible method should be considered. Experiments over a period of years have proved that you will benefit from use of alpha tocopherol, a form of vitamin E. Herbert Bailey wrote: "A natural anti-oxidant and oxygen-conservator such as vitamin E affords the body many advantages. . . The heart muscle itself is more richly nourished with oxygen through its main source of blood supply, the coronary arteries. These two factors — less work and more oxygen — partially explain why the vitamin has a direct, beneficial, seemingly miraculous effect on flagging hearts, and on normal hearts as well. Researchers have stated that vitamin E therapy is equivalent to being placed in an oxygen tent — without the inconvenience, of course."[9]

HOW TO CARRY MORE BLOOD TO YOUR MUSCLES

Your blood is forced through smaller and smaller arteries until it reaches capillaries so small that only one cell at a time can squeeze through. This red blood cell takes more than a second to pass through a capillary one-half millimeter long. In that time oxygen diffuses through the membrane into cells in the muscle fiber.

Capillaries consist mainly of endothelium, a single, thin layer of cells forming a membrane through which oxygen, food and other necessities can reach your muscle cells. Endothelium reproduces itself in a few days, and so new openings soon have a lining of endothelial cells.

Capillaries have no smooth muscles, and so they cannot open and close like arteries. But, "The arteriovenous anastomoses are vessels, the walls of which consist almost entirely of smooth muscle. They serve as a direct connection between the arteries and veins, bypassing the capillaries. . . If an organ is active, the anastomoses close and the blood may flow through the capillaries, whereas in a resting organ the anastomoses may open and let the blood bypass the capillaries."[8]

Thus, more blood is forced through capillaries where it is needed simply by shutting down areas with lower priority.

Toni Nett quotes Professor Joseph Nocker: "For endurance performance, resistance to fatigue is the decisive factor. The capacity for taking in oxygen, therefore, plays a leading part. The ability to take in oxygen, on the other hand, is closely coupled with the superficial blood-vessel system, particularly the capillaries. Thus it is to be understood that the first reaction of a muscle trained for endurance is an increase in the capacity for complete blood suffusion (supplying blood to muscles) through an increase in capillaries. Investigations of rabbit muscles have shown that not only are more capillaries formed, but that cross-connections between the capillaries have also increased. A substantially improved oxygen exchange is thereby made possible. If one were to try to grasp the change quantitatively, one would find that there is a doubling of capillaries per muscle fiber and the connections between the capillaries increase as much as three and one-half fold. Thus every muscle fiber is surrounded by a thicker network of capillaries. Along with the intensified capillarization, there is also an increase in the total diameter, which results in a slower blood flow. This prolongs the contact between the blood and the tissue so that oxygen is delivered in larger quantities."[93]

Physiologists counted 1050 open capillaries in one square millimeter of a dog's muscle. (There are more than 600 square millimeters in a square inch.) In the exercised muscle, they found 2010 open capillaries. This was in an area that would hold 1690 muscle fibers, and they did not count cross-connecting capillaries. Thus, in a trained muscle, you have more capillaries than muscle fibers.

There is considerable physiological proof that improved vascularization (more capillaries) is necessary for great endurance. In one type of experiment, the blood supply is cut off from one side of your body (in a finger, for example). After a training period, your free finger has far more stamina than the one trained without a blood supply.

The most sensational demonstration of the value of capillaries (plus muscle metabolism) can be seen in a man who is in excellent condition for an endurance event. Take, for example, a champion swimmer in top shape, and put him on a running track. He knows how to run, from his boyhood play, but he is unable to compete with trained runners even though he has a well-trained respiratory system, a large and strong heart and an extra supply of red blood cells and hemoglobin. He can do a great job of supplying his swimming muscles with oxygen, but he cannot do the same for his running muscles.

His running muscles simply do not receive enough oxygen. In trained muscles, more and more capillaries begin to function. Existing capillaries are enlarged. Vestigial capillaries are forced open and used regularly. And physiologists say you can actually open new capillaries. Dr. Benjamin Zweifach calls capillaries nothing more than tunnels, and he says they are probably the same structurally as the tissue around them, with the addition of endothelial cells.[149]

Of all the means to carry oxygen to your muscles, by far the largest improvement can be made in your system of capillaries around your muscle fibers. You cannot possibly be a distance runner unless you force your capillaries open.

One physiologist said, "The blood flow through maximally working muscles must be 50 or more times greater than in rest."[2] Since your cardiac output can account for an increase of only five or six times your resting volume of blood, your vascular system must increase blood flow in the working muscles about ten-fold.

One specific experiment with catheters brought this conclusion: "The calculated blood flow through the exercising leg increased about ten-fold with heavy work."[18]

This seemingly miraculous effect is accomplished by two methods:

• Almost immediately after muscles begin contracting, the nearby capillaries open.

• Other organs and muscles in the body shut down their capillaries so that little oxygen is wasted.

This is a natural regulation of your body, no matter how well trained you are. But if the tiny capillaries around your working muscle fibers are not able to transport red blood cells, your muscles will not receive oxygen. The saturated blood will merely run through your anastomoses into your veins.

Thus, whether or not you make use of your wonderful oxygen transport system depends entirely upon the capillaries near your working muscle fibers. The oxygen-carrying capacity of these capillaries can be increased greatly.

The need for oxygen stimulates increased capillarization. Experiments with rats and rabbits at a simulated altitude of 20,000 to 25,000 feet for several months showed a doubling of the diameter of capillaries in their brains.[32]

Krogh concluded that "the flow of blood to active organs is increased by some reaction on the part of the active tissue itself. . . The tissue cells will under a number of stimuli liberate substances having a dilator action on their smallest blood vessels."[68]

Thus, somehow or other in a way not yet clear, more capillaries tunnel their way through tissues and are eventually lined with endothelium. "The elastic properties of the capillaries and of the tissue were identical. Therefore, they must be the same structurally, and probably are one and the same thing."[149]

Any type of training increases vascularization, but continuous exercise is best. Severe exercise, such as sprinting, probably does not produce much capillarization because your muscles contract tightly and prevent blood from flowing.[66]

Lydiard said, "The Germans in Cologne did tests on endurance runners in 1969 and found that if you work any muscle group for two hours without stopping, you get greater muscular capillarization. Not only do you quickly develop underdeveloped capillary beds, but you develop new capillary beds. This transports more oxygen to the muscles. So just by keeping these muscles going for a long period of time, we developed greater muscular endurance. . . Someone might run one and one-half hours faster than you run two and one-half hours, but you'll get better muscular capillarization."[50]

It seems probable that good capillarization takes place in borderline running, because you can continue longer.

Dr. Hollmann wrote: "The stimulus for new formation of the capillaries appears to be the lack of oxygen or the acidification of the tissue such as occurs at the beginning of a physical exertion. In analogy to other observations in muscle physiology and in the clinic, the fact seems to obtain here also that mode-rate stimuli produce stimui of optimal (most favorable) influence on capillarization while too mild or too strong stimuli may actually have a deleterious effect."[93]

Thus, capillarization calls for only one addition to your training program: You must exercise every muscle you might possibly need. This means you should run on your toes in some of your long continuous runs, even though your competitive stride is nearer flat-footed. You should do some running with a longer stride than normal, and some with a shorter stride. You should lift your knees higher than normally for many miles so as to develop capillaries in those muscles. You should swing your arms excessively part of the time. If you add all possible capillaries to all possible running muscles, you will avoid unnecessary limitations that could cost you a race.

If you take alpha tocopherol, you may also receive help with your capillarization. Bert Bailey wrote: "Vitamin E is also a vasodilator: It opens arteries (particularly those all-important smallest ones, the arterioles) so that more blood can flow through the circulatory system." And he quotes the Darlington-Chassels Report about the place of alpha tocopherol in improvement in race horses: "It enables the tissues of the body to do the same job on less oxygen; it is as if one strapped an aqua-lung (with oxygen) on the horse's back. It opens up huge reserves of capillary circulation, sets of vessels not ordinarily used but waiting there for emergency demands."[9]

HOW TO GET THE MOST ENERGY FROM YOUR MUSCLE CELLS

The energy produced inside your muscle cells is both aerobic and anaerobic, and there is a definite connection between their activities. It is not as if you use energy from one gas tank and then switch over to another, but rather a complicated mixture in one tank.

Inside your muscle cells, action of almost incredible complexity takes place. Many books could be written about what goes on within a single cell, but here we are only interested in activities that influence your endurance. Here, grossly simplified, are the basic biochemical activities that relate to endurance:

Energy from the sun is in the food you eat. The chemical form this energy takes in your body is glucose, obtained mostly from the starches and sugars of carbohydrates. Glucose enters your bloodstream through your intestines and circulates, ready for use. Some of it is changed into glycogen, which may be up to 30,000 glucose molecules linked together by withdrawal of water. Glycogen is the form in which energy is stored in your muscles, and in your liver, where it can be changed back into glucose when you need it. (Energy from fats is used during moderate exercise and when carbohydrate energy begins to run out; energy from proteins is used in emergencies.)

Glucose in your muscle cell is broken down chemically into carbon dioxide (a poisonous gas that you later exhale), plus water and energy. Part of that energy is stored in a compound called adenosine triphosphate (ATP). This ATP is bound together by high-energy bonds. When these molecular bonds are split, energy is released to contract your muscles. Your ability to move depends upon the presence of ATP in the mitochondria of your cells.

Unfortunately, your supply of ATP is used up in about one-half second. You must continually rebuild it in order to keep running. Your ATP supply can be rebuilt in three ways:

• Part of the energy from glucose is stored as creatine phosphate (CP) in your muscles. After ATP splits off one of its three phosphate groups to create energy, it becomes adenosine diphosphate (ADP). CP can transfer its phosphate to ADP, which then becomes ATP again.[12] (This method of rebuilding ATP can increase your immediate supply of muscle energy several times. It is an anaerobic method *without* producing lactic acid and it lasts only a few seconds during hard running.)

• Glucose in your muscle cell goes through six chemical changes during glycolysis until it becomes pyruvic acid. Most of this pyruvic acid goes into a series of reactions called the Krebs Cycle (also called citric acid cycle or tricarboxylic acid cycle). But if there is a shortage of oxygen, some of it changes to lactic acid, yielding more ATP. The lactic acid is stored temporarily in the cell. (Many things can happen to this lactic acid, and some of them can cause you trouble. This will be the subject of the chapter about anaerobic endurance.)

But some lactic acid reverses the process and oxidizes (by loss of hydrogen) into pyruvic acid. This reversal of glycolytic reactions within your skeletal muscles costs you the loss of two high-energy bonds. This fact — that your anaerobic mechanism is partially reversible — is one reason why it is impossible to separate completely the aerobic and anaerobic systems.

• The third system for rebuilding ATP is the aerobic way (oxidative phosphorylation). The Krebs Cycle is the main pathway for the final oxidation of the products of carbohydrates, fats and proteins. To make a highly complex story short. . . pyruvic acid enters the Krebs Cycle instead of becoming lactic acid. Hydrogen breaks off from the Krebs Cycle in your mitochondria to the cytochromes. This is where fresh oxygen enters biological oxidation for the first time. Water is formed and enters the cytoplasm of your cell, where carbon dioxide also goes from the Krebs Cycle. ATP is delivered from the cytochrome system to the mitochondria at a rate of 14 ATP molecules from oxidation of each pyruvate molecule. About 90 percent of all your ATP is produced here.

Your first movements are anaerobic without lactic acid (alactacid), except for some oxygen stored in your muscle cells. Next, you produce pyruvic acid, which is either broken down into lactic acid or enters the Krebs Cycle to produce ATP with the use of oxygen. To complicate matters further, both actions can take place at once. And lactic acid, which is supposed to indicate anaerobic energy, disappears during your "steady state." In fact, your oxygen debt can be used at any time during your race. If all the facts were known, it is probable that aerobic and anaerobic energy production are not only intertwined in their mechanisms, but they actually help each other. For that reason, and because anaerobic endurance is the subject of a separate discussion, only the obviously aerobic mechanisms are considered here.

The important question: Can your cells use all the oxygen available, or is it your cells that limit your endurance?

Tests on top athletes[40] show that they reach their maximum cardiac outputs with their maximum oxygen uptake. This seems to indicate that their oxygen transport system limits their oxygen uptake. But athletes can perform more work with far less blood flow than untrained men. This proves that their cells utilize more oxygen.

A study of the figures in those same tests show that good athletes can utilize about 90 percent of all the oxygen that reaches their capillaries. Two athletes used 96 percent. Asmussen wrote this about utilization of oxygen: "In heavy exercise it must reach values close to the total arterial oxygen capacity."[3]

This ability to use all the available oxygen does not come naturally to your cells, however, for several physiologists have reported increases from training or living at high altitudes. This improvement in the capacity of your cells to use oxygen takes place in several areas:

Myoglobin. Inside your muscle cells, myoglobin carries oxygen much the way hemoglobin does in your bloodstream. The supply of oxygen in trained men has been calculated as high as 0.43 liters, enough for several seconds of running. The instant your muscle cell contracts, the myoglobin begins to release oxygen.[115] Thus, aerobic action follows close behind or actually combines with the instant alactacid energy. (This is part of the complicated difference between aerobic and anaerobic energy mentioned previously.)

In addition to storing oxygen for your use when needed, myoglobin acts as a catalyst of oxidizing processes. Many tests show increases in myoglobin from training. Rats who were trained hard for 12 weeks showed 80 percent more myoglobin in their running muscles.[99] Myoglobin increases when you live at high altitudes. "Rats acclimatized to high altitude and made to run on a treadmill developed 50 percent more myoglobin than similar animals trained at sea level."[76]

Mitochondria. Your mitochondria and mitochondrial enzymes are capable of oxidizing pyruvate, and thus they release 90 percent of the energy you use for aerobic running. Rats who were trained extensively doubled their capacity to utilize the oxygen that reached their cells.[52] They had 60 percent more protein in their mitochondria.

Phosphocreatine. Your fastest method of replenishing your supply of ATP is from creatine phosphate (CP) in the alactacid process. Margaria estimates about 90 to 135 calories of energy per kilogram of body weight are available in CP stored in your muscles. This is enough energy to run a hundred yards. CP storage increases with training.

No evidence is available to prove which kind of training is best to make your cells function at their highest capacity. Probably whatever *endurance* training you do will stimulate your cells to increase their capacity. Almost certainly, they will keep up with any increase you can make in supplying them with oxygen.

Once again, Herbert Bailey points out the possibilities of alpha tocopherol: "When richly supplied with vitamin E, the cells of the body are able to perform more efficiently — not demanding as much oxygen for metabolic processes, thereby freeing more oxygen for those cells and organs needing it."[9]

HOW TO INCREASE YOUR SUPPLY OF GLYCOGEN

You cannot run as well without a large glycogen supply. The glucose in your blood amounts to only about 3 percent of the glycogen you can store in your liver, and so you would run out of energy very soon without glycogen.

Glycogen in your liver is readily changed back to glucose as you need it, but your total supply of glycogen is definitely limited. An average amount of glycogen in your body would weigh about one and one-half pounds. About one-third is stored in your liver and most of the rest is stored in your muscles.

It is true that when you run short of glycogen you can burn fat instead. In the Harvard Fatigue Laboratory, "a fasting dog ran for 27 hours and performed 10 times as much work as could be accounted for by the glycogen reserves in his body. As the carbohydrate reserve diminishes, the proportion of energy derived from fat may increase from 8 to 77 percent."[64]

The physiological factor used to determine what percentage of your energy comes from glycogen is your respiratory quotient (RQ). This is simply a comparison of the amount of carbon dioxide you exhale compared to the amount of oxygen you use.

When the small amount of protein metabolism is subtracted or disregarded, and carbon dioxide equals oxygen, your RQ is 1.0, which means you are burning 100 percent carbohydrate. When carbon dioxide is only 70 percent as much as oxygen, your RQ is 0.70, which means you are burning 100 percent fat. The percentage of carbohydrate you are burning can be calculated in between those extremes. An RQ of 0.85 is considered normal — 49 percent carbohydrates.

It is difficult to calculate exactly how much time you will lose in a race from a depletion of your glycogen reserves. At an RQ of 1.00, each liter of oxygen produces 5.047 kilocalories. At an RQ of 0.85, a liter of oxygen produces only 4.863, and at 0.70 it produces only 4.686. In a treadmill 10,000-meter run, a runner was burning about 73 percent carbohydrate at the halfway point and 53 percent at the finish. Calculating only the reduction in energy for the change in carbohydrates, he was forced to run 1 percent slower for the second 5000 meters — a loss of about nine seconds.

But physiologists have estimated the loss of *efficiency* as 5 to 15 percent. Perhaps the loss of running skill plus the build-up of metabolites from burning fats causes a far greater loss of time.

To understand this problem of fuel supply, you must distinguish between glycogen stored in your muscles and all the rest of the glucose in your body (including liver glycogen, which turns into glucose in order to enter your bloodstream on its way to your muscles). Muscle glycogen cannot be used to form blood glucose.

It is easy to see some of the results of a shortage of glucose:

• When you no longer have enough glucose, it shows in tests as low blood sugar. Karpovich reported on the 1924 Boston Marathon: "While, before the race, their blood sugars ranged between 81 and 108 milligrams, at the finish, there was a marked difference. The winner had a comparatively normal blood sugar and was in excellent condition. Four of the runners had 50, 49, 47, and 45 milligrams, respectively. Three of them were completely exhausted, and the fourth was unconscious and had to be carried."[64]

• Tests show that the human body prefers to burn carbohydrates, and when your workload is heavy, your RQ is high. This burning of carbohydrates remains high in trained athletes until "the organism's glycogen depots are reduced too much, the subject is obliged to decrease his work intensity or, if he has a strong will, he can work with the same high load until he collapses."[47]

• Experiments[3] show that after three days on a fat diet a man was exhausted after an hour and a half (at an expenditure of about two and one-half liters of oxygen per minute). The same man on a carbohydrate diet did the same work for four hours *without* exhaustion.

• "The low blood sugar resulting from depleting the carbohydrate stores may influence the central nervous system and thus the coordinated muscular performance."[3] Thus, when you burn fat, you lose part of your running skill, which means both loss of speed and greater inefficiency in your use of oxygen.

Depletion of the glycogen supply in your muscles causes additional types of fatigue:

• "Under the present circulatory conditions the duration of exercise does not appear to be limited by circulatory or respiratory functions. . . A close correlation was found between performance time and initial muscle glycogen content. There was also a fair correlation between muscle glycogen decrease and performance time. . . . All these correlations indicate that the local glycogen store in the working muscles is a determining factor for the ability to perform long-term exercise, i.e., the higher the muscle glycogen content, the longer the performance time. . . It has recently been shown that the glycogen concentration is critical for the resyntheses of phosphorylcreatine and ATP in the working muscles in man."[1]

These tests show that glycogen in muscles was used at a certain rate, even though added glucose was available. Ahlborg calls it "an obligatory breakdown of muscle glycogen." Therefore, "the muscle glycogen content is an important limiting factor in the ability to also perform exercise when the blood glucose concentration is high. It thus appears as though the metabolism of added glucose replaces, to a great extent, the fat combustion during work, but cannot replace the energy derived from muscle glycogen."[1]

Astrand showed that when muscle glycogen stores were low (as a result of diet), men could perform a certain workload for only one hour. When the muscle glycogen stores were four times as high, they could perform the same work for four hours.[6]

• "Fat alone cannot be burned efficiently without sugar. Certain acids and acetone, formed from incompletely utilized fat, accumulate in the body and cause acetone acidosis. . . Even mild acidosis can cause fatigue, nervousness, headache, and nausea."[30] The salts formed could well be part of the cause of tight and sore legs after long runs.

• With no glycogen to convert to lactic acid, your anaerobic capacity dwindles, leaving you without a reserve for the final drive in a race. "It is interesting to find that cross-country skiers who have raced about 50 kilometers (32 miles) and then perform exhausting exercise on a bicycle or treadmill can hardly produce any lactic acid."[7]

Physiologists have found various reasons why the presence of glycogen in your running muscles enables you to continue running for a longer time. You do have a net gain of one high-energy bond when you start with muscle glycogen instead of blood glucose, but this depletes your supply. One possible reason is that glycogen is already in your muscle cell, while glucose must be transported through the cell membrane, and so glucose is somewhat less efficient.[61]

Another reason is that in order to burn fat effectively, you need some sugar. Still another reason is that your brain and nervous system reserve a supply of glucose for themselves. Since you cannot live without such glucose, your body cleverly inhibits glucose from entering muscle cells when blood glucose runs low.

Whatever the reason, you need to increase storage of glycogen in your muscles if you want to run long distances well.

You can do three things to increase your glycogen supply: train, eat and rest. These must be done in the right way and in a certain combination to obtain best results.

Bergstrom proved that diet alone has effect upon your glycogen supply. Glycogen content (per 100 grams of wet muscle) varied as follows:

After a normal mixed diet = 1.75 grams.
After three days of high-fat, high-protein diet = 0.6 grams.
After three days on a carbohydrate-rich diet = 3.5 grams.

Their ability to work dropped from 114 minutes to 60, then shot up to 170 minutes.

An experiment on two men provides scientific evidence that exercise and diet combined will do even better. The two men sat on either side of a bicycle ergometer, so that one used his left leg and the other used his right leg. Their other legs remained at rest. They pumped for five to 20 minutes at a time and rested for a like amount. They continued until they were so exhausted they could not pump for longer than one minute.

Then biopsies were taken from the extensor muscles of their thighs. The glycogen content of their exercised legs was almost zero. Their rested legs contained the normal amount of glycogen. For three days they were fed a diet of carbohydrates with dramatic results. While biopsies of their rested legs showed a small increase in glycogen content, their exercised legs continued to store glycogen until, after three days, their glycogen content was double that of their rested legs.

Astrand and Rodahl report: "It was further observed that the most pronounced effect was obtained if the glycogen depots were first emptied by heavy, prolonged exercise and then maintained low by giving the subject a diet low in carbohydrate, followed by a few days with a diet rich in carbohydrates. With this procedure the glycogen content could exceed 4 gm/100 gm wet muscle."[4] This was an added improvement of almost 15 percent simply by withholding carbohydrates temporarily.

Other physiologists have reported this supercompensation in glycogen storage after exercise. An experiment on rabbits produced three times as much glycogen after several weeks, and an increase of two or three times in three to 15 days has been reported.[76]

This method is now used by marathoners and called "carbohydrate-loading": 1) Exhaust yourself. 2) Eat a low-carbohydrate diet for three days. 3) Eat a high-carbohydrate diet for three days.

However, there are warnings about carbo-loading. First, it adds up to four pounds of water and makes you stiff. There have been reports of infections, emotional instability, angina and one heart attack while running. In addition, some runners have performed poorly after loading.

Many experts find fault with the excess of protein and fat in the low-carbohydrate period. No harm will come to you if you eliminate this period. Eat normally instead, then eat only carbohydrates for the last three days. You gain from carbohydrate-loading only in races that last more than an hour.

Arthur Lydiard recognizes the value of the exhausting long run: "If I flogged myself one day, even to the point of exhaustion, even to the point where I had to walk or shamble, I would recover sufficiently to continue easier work in the following days, and a week to ten days after the exhaustion run I would become markedly stronger."[77]

Conflicting statements are made about how you can best increase your glycogen supply by training. Some say only long runs[129] will do it, while others advocate anaerobic training.[35]

Probably any running that exhausts your glycogen supply will stimulate a larger storage of glycogen. Normally, this is thought to take two and one-half hours.[84] But faster running burns glycogen faster. A large dose of anaerobic running, however, results in some replenishment of glycogen within the cell, and so this may not be as great a stimulant to glycogen reserves as a long run to exhaustion.

If long, exhausting runs are necessary, you can get some of this training in races, if you are a long distance runner who races 20 or more times a year. But if your races are bunched into one part of the year, or you run shorter distances, you probably need some long training runs.

These should emphasize length of time, not speed. You can recognize the symptoms of glycogen shortage after many miles at an easy pace. Without feeling any "aerobic stress," you begin to notice a lack of spring in your legs, then a tightening of certain muscles, developing into pain. You should stop when the pain appears.

A simple way of increasing your glycogen supply is through the food you eat. A diet heavy in fat and protein will reduce your glycogen reserves. A diet heavy in carbohydrates will increase your glycogen supply. This does not mean you should eat only carbohydrates, for there are other considerations. It does mean that before and after long runs you should increase your carbohydrate intake. This is done both to increase your glycogen reserves and to build up your glucose supply for an immediate effort.

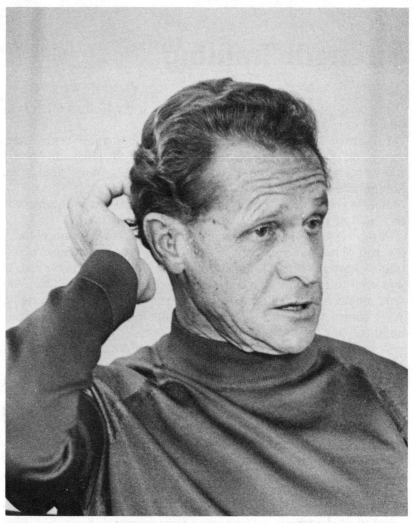

Arthur Lydiard is perhaps the world's most famed running coach who preaches long, slow distance. He has coached such successful Olympians as Peter Snell (gold medal in the 800), Murray Halberg, Bill Baillie and Barry Maggee.

4

Strength Training

It is easy to increase your strength, but will added strength help you become a better runner?

It is obvious that you must develop your running muscles in order to run. At the other extreme, it is obvious that the large and powerful torso of a 250-pound shot putter would only slow you. Somewhere in between lies your answer.

Before you attempt a final answer, you should review the elementary anatomy and physiology of muscular strength.

A muscle is a wonderful machine that performs mechanical tasks for you. Through a complicated chemical process, a muscle contracts (shortens) when stimulated by an impulse from a nerve cell. If you want to raise your hand from your side to touch your face, you send an electrical impulse to your biceps and that muscle shortens. As it contracts, it pulls the bone of your lower arm, raising your hand to your face.

A muscle is composed of thousands of individual muscle fibers, bundled together by connective tissue in groups of 100 to 150. A cross-section of muscle an inch wide might have 20 to 200 such groups bound together in larger and larger units.

You have control over the amount of contraction in individual (voluntary) muscles. If not, your hand would fly up and slap your face with maximum force instead of rising slowly. This control is possible because separate groups (motor units) operate independently, activated by a single motor nerve fiber. Although every fiber in that group contracts at once, other groups remain idle until needed. There is also a difference in force because of the rapidity of the impulses from your motor nerve cells.

If you want to lift a weight in your hand, you send more impulses to make more muscle groups contract. If the weight is so heavy that all muscle groups, with each impulse at maximum frequency, cannot lift it, then you need more strength.

You can develop more strength by contracting a muscle against resistance. This means the harder you use a muscle, the stronger it grows.

For example, suppose you want to develop the muscles that lift your knee higher while running. Ordinary running strengthens those muscles. Running with an exaggerated knee lift strengthens them further. Lifting your knee with a weight tied to your foot will develop much more strength.

Physiologists disagree as to exactly what happens when you increase your strength. Many accept the theory that your individual muscle fibers thicken as they become stronger. Others, however, point out that hypertrophy (increase in size) of a muscle can be the result of a large increase in the number of small blood vessels (capillaries), of a thickening of the membranes (sarcolemma) around each fiber, of an increase in connective tissue, and of increase in chemical content. Many coaches know that strength can increase greatly without any observable increase in muscle size, although this might be because an exercised muscle is surrounded by less fat.

Throughout the track world, arguments rage about the value of strength training for runners. Arthur Lydiard, coach of Peter Snell and Murray Halberg, among others, said, "My athletes never do weight training. What do they want with bulky, bunchy lifting muscles, however impressive they may be? They don't need big muscles, only supple, strong muscles. . . You don't want muscles like an ox; you want muscles like a deer — stretched, supple, relaxed, splendidly conditioned. . . by running."[77]

At the opposite extreme is Percy Cerutty, coach of Herb Elliott. Cerutty believed a runner is greatly improved by all-around strength and power. He said, ". . . we can so strengthen an athlete, such as Elliott, so that which appears abnormal to others becomes normal for him merely because he has acquired greatly added strength . . . Indeed, I am convinced that for future superior performances running alone can never be the answer."[21]

First, consider the possible disadvantages some people claim for strength training:

1) If it increases your weight in muscles not used to propel you in running, you cannot run as fast.

2) A stronger muscle is slower.

3) A stronger muscle has less endurance.

Cantankerous, unorthodox. These words describe Percy Cerutty, left, the enigmatic Australian coach who gained fame from his training methods and camp at Portsea. Herb Elliott, right, 1500-meter gold-medal winner, was one of Cerutty's proteges.

4) Weight training takes a lot of time, which would best be devoted to running.

5) Injuries are possible.

Against these disadvantages, consider the claims *for* weight training:

a) If your running muscles are stronger, you can run at a given speed with less effort or at a greater speed with the same effort.

b) Certain weight training programs increase endurance.

c) Many parts of your body are not strengthened by running, and this weakness slows you in an all-out race. If you are stronger, you are a more powerful runner.

Which of the above claims are true?

1) is absolutely true. If you develop your strength until you are the size of a shot putter or weightlifter, you will be too heavy to run well.

You can, however, develop strength in several ways without

adding weight where you cannot use it:

• Overloaded running is strength training. (Sprints, uphill running and running with weights.)

• Weight training with light weights and many repetitions develops less bulk.

• If only the running muscles are developed, they will more than carry their weight. In addition, running will hold them to a reasonable size.

• If any part of your body begins to develop too much, you can reduce it simply by discontinuing your weightlifting.

2) is sometimes true. Some physiologists have demonstrated that stronger muscles are slower. A.W. Korobkov, brother of Gavriil Korobkov, former head coach of the USSR track team, claims: "When heavy loads were used right from the start, the tests without load indicated increased strength in the trained muscle groups but decrease in the speed of movement."

Other physiologists dispute this. Three West Germans stated: "There is a widespread opinion that the speed of contraction is impeded by excessive muscular growth (hypertrophy). Zorbas and Karpovich were able to prove the contrary to be true. Weightlifters possessed greater rotational speed of the arms than ordinary persons." [111]

And Korobkov adds: "Continuous training with light loads developed all movement components (speed, strength, endurance) much better."

Perhaps any fault lies in overdevelopment of the wrong muscles. If you are careful in that respect, you need not worry about losing speed.

3) is also true. . . . if hypertrophy is overdone. You *can* lessen endurance by building too much muscle mass. Korobkov stated: "Too much strength training, as a rule, leads to an increase in the muscle mass (increased weight), to an unfavorable oxygen supply to muscles, and to a restricted fluency in movement."

If you are a runner, it is important to avoid any increase in the size and weight of muscles developed by weight training.

4) is not necessarily true. Weight training can be squeezed in unless you are unusually pressed for time. But is it worth it?

Arthur Lydiard said, "I doubt if Halberg lifted 20 pounds above his head in his life and I am quite certain that, even if he had, he wouldn't have been any faster as a runner." [77]

A British coach strongly in favor of weight training is Tony

Ward: "Often time is an important factor and in this case the runner should divide his strength training throughout the week, accompanying running sessions with one or two exercises at a time. . . The old argument that time spent weight training could be spent, and should be spent, running is, of course, so much nonsense. Much of the running which takes place toward the end of a training session is of no value anyway, and the mental boost of engaging in another activity is often invaluable after a hard running session."[139]

John Jesse wrote: "The time factor probably represents the greatest objection that most track coaches have against a separate strength development program. They counter this objection by combining strength training with speed or endurance training. . . The objective of the runner is to win the race in the fastest time, not to become the strongest man in the race.

"The time spent by an athlete in learning some semblance of the basic skills, coordination, timing, and balance required for Olympic lifting movements could be better spent in developing strength in those muscles primarily used by him in his specialty. . . . Why should a runner who, through gymnastics or other means, has developed enough strength in his arms and shoulders to chin himself 15 or 20 times and do 20 to 25 dips on the parallel bars, spend his time on weight training exercises for those areas of the body?"[60]

The answer would seem to be that weight training *can* be overdone and, if so, it is too time consuming. On the other hand, it can be held to a minimum of extra time in several ways:

• Do not waste time becoming a fully skilled Olympic-type weightlifter. A runner does not need the skills, nor the strength.

• Combine strength training with resistance running for speed and endurance.

• Be an efficiency engineer in your use of time. Do the bulk of your weight training during the off season. Spread it out over the whole week so you won't need one long session on any single day. Fit it into rest periods between runs or sets of runs, as did Jim Ryun.[88]

• On any day you simply do not have time, choose running over weight training.

5) is possible. You *can* injure yourself while using weights.

Dr. P.R. Travers discusses this aspect of weight training: "In general, the more complex the skills involved in any particular exercises, the greater the risk of injury. If this were the end of the matter, I would hesitate to recommend weight training to athletes. Fortunately, however, it is possible to train with weights and never to use any complicated skills at all. In other words, perfectly adequate schedules can be built up by using simple primary joint exercises in which relatively few muscle groups are exercised in turn."[132]

If you want to improve your running through strength training, you should be coached by someone with knowledge in both sports. You must specialize in weight training that will help you as a runner. And you must obey all the safety rules.

Now, let's consider the claims *for* weight training:

a) is true. If all else is equal, stronger running muscles enable you to run faster.

Frank Sevigne, University of Nebraska coach of Charlie Greene, wrote: "The main problem we are concerned with is the increase of stride length. This can mainly be done with an increase of leg strength. . . By improving leg, foot and ankle strength. . . We are looking for a powerful, explosive thrust of the driving or rear leg, ankle and foot. The stronger and more explosive the force of the driving leg, the greater the stride length and the greater the thrust."

Sevigne was discussing sprinters, but the same principle applies to long-distance runners. Consider this arithmetic: If all else is equal, and a miler develops enough added strength to add an inch to each stride without using extra energy, he would run the mile about three seconds faster.

Dr. Clayne R. Jensen of Brigham Young University points out that "running speed is closely related to power because running is nothing more than a series of body projections made alternately from the right and left feet. In running, the body is propelled forward by the force applied by the body levers against a resistance (the surface). If all else remains equal, increased strength will cause increased application of force, which may result in improved running speed."[58]

There seems to be no question: Strength can increase speed.

b) is true. Strength training can increase endurance.

In the first place, any increase in speed equals an increase in endurance because you use fewer muscle fibers to run at the same pace.

Morehouse and Miller confirm this: "The strength of the working muscles is a limiting factor in endurance. A load easily carried by a strong muscle may quickly exhaust weak ones. When a strong muscle lifts a comparatively light load only a relatively few fibers need to be brought into play. As these become fatigued, their threshold of irritability is raised, and they fail to respond to the stimuli. The stimuli then arouse fresh fibers and they take over the work, while the fatigued fibers recuperate in order to resume the burden later on if necessary."[84]

Jensen agrees: "Strength is also a basic component of muscular endurance. Endurance is defined as the ability to resist fatigue and to recover quickly after fatigue. It implies that an athlete can persist in his performance at a given level. If a weak muscle can perform a movement against a given resistance fifty times, then a stronger muscle could perform against the same resistance with greater ease and, therefore, could repeat the movement considerably more than fifty times."[58]

Dr. Ellington Darden, who improved two Boston Marathon runners through weight training, said, "If you strengthen the right muscles, I'll guarantee you'll improve your running ability. And it doesn't matter if you're a sprinter or a marathoner, Olympic champion or novice, male or female, 15 or 50."[29]

You must, of course, add strength in the proper places and in the proper amount. Overdevelopment of upper body strength detracts from running endurance, because you weigh more with no gain in running power. Overdevelopment of your running muscles detracts, as stated.

In choosing types and methods of weight training, then, it would seem as if you should use lighter weights with more repetitions to emphasize endurance while gaining in strength.

c) is debatable. This is the Lydiard vs. Cerutty controversy all over again, and no real conclusion has been reached.

Dr. Woldemar Gerschler, the famous German coach, believes special training is necessary for the chest and back as well as the legs. Probably a large majority of coaches agree.

Dr. Hollmann of Germany points out that the protective tissue that bundles groups of muscle fiber together is weakened by continuous running. This makes it easy to injure the muscle. The solution is strength training for the muscle.

Fred Wilt says, "Strength is the athlete's capacity to exert muscular force against resistance. With increased strength, greater power (rate of work) can be developed. Thus, with all other factors equal, the stronger runner should win."[142]

Tony Ward wrote: "I believe that this will be a most important facet of training for the middle-distance runner of the future — that the 13-minute three-miler will have to possess a high weight to strength ratio, as well as endurance."[139]

Jesse gives a more specific reason for strengthening upper body muscles: "The spine is a single weight bearing column that depends entirely upon muscular strength for both lateral and anterior-posterior stabilization. As a person sways back and forth, the abdominal and spinal muscles contract alternately to correct the resulting displacement of the trunk from the vertical and modify the force of the gravitational pull. The slight body lean (5 to 9 degrees) of the distance runner creates a tension in the posterior trunk muscles for periods of four minutes to two hours, depending on the event. A lack of strength in the spinal muscles contributes to fatigue in this body area, which may cause an alteration in running style, a loss of efficiency, and an overall feeling of body fatigue."[60]

The evidence, mostly empirical, seems to favor increased body strength. But the fact that some runners have broken world records without weight training indicates this value plays a relatively small part in running success. On the other hand, who knows how much faster they might have run with extra strength? If you want to use the shotgun principle by trying everything, then you certainly must develop your upper body as well as your legs.

If you decide to use strength training, you must first consider four types of strength work: exercises, isometrics, resistance running, and weight training.

1) Exercises

Exercises, such as calisthenics or gymnastics, are used for stretching, flexibility, and warmups as well as for strengthening.

Lydiard says, "The most important exercises are those that tone up the stomach muscles, chiefly by back-bending. These muscles are more essential to the middle- and long-distance runner than any other in the body apart from the legs."[77]

Various types of sit-ups will strenghten your important abdominal muscles.

One of the main objections to using exercises for strengthening is that they lack the progressive overload of weight training. On the other hand, since runners do not need maximum strength, these exercises may be sufficient.

2) Isometrics

In isometric contractions you exert muscular power against a stationary object (such as a fixed bar).

Isometric contractions can be of value, but there are many drawbacks: Your strongest muscles will show the least gain. You develop strength only at the point where you exert the force instead

of through the full range of movement. An extreme effort is required, but it demonstrates no immediate results and injuries are
possible.

Isometrics can help you most as a supplement when you lack time
or equipment for other strength training.

3) Resistance Running

Resistance running is another kind of exercise, but it is placed in a
separate group because it simulates the running movement. Its object is to develop strength in your running muscles at the same time
it develops muscle endurance.

Resistance running cannot be measured as accurately as weight
training, but it has the advantage of being a running movement.
Tadeusz Kepka, national coach of middle-distance runners in
Poland, claims, "All kinds of running up steep slopes in deep snow,
as well as long-distance mountain hikes (up to 30 kilometers in four
hours of non-stop marching) gives the runner something indispensable in terms of strength in his legs and hips. This cannot be obtained by indoor calisthenics."

When you consider that endurance is more important than
strength, you must weigh the advantages of doing strength training
with a running movement. You can use a tremendous variety of
resistance running exercises. In fact, they seem to be restricted only
by the limits of human ingenuity. Here are some:

• Exaggerated movements (no resistance except yourself). Sprinting is a form of resistance running for distance runners. Other exag-
gerations are high knee lift, extremely fast and short steps, and
bounding (long, slow strides).

• Running with weights (vest, belt, shoes, leg weights), such as
Zatopek's running in heavy boots.

• Running against the resistance of a belt held back by another
runner.

• Running against the resistance of gravity: up hills, stairs or
steps. Many coaches advocate hill running of various types.

• Running against the resistance of the surface (snow, shallow
water, fields of grass, sand).

• Combinations. Lydiard, for example, strongly advises springing
or bounding up a hill rather than running up. Herb Elliott
popularized sandhill running. Hill or stair running can be made progressively harder by adding weighted belts or vests.

4) Weight Training

By using weights, you can develop more strength in any of your muscles, and you can do it faster.

Most weight training is done with a barbell, dumbbells, or an expensive machine, but you can improvise with wall pulleys, weighted containers (such as a sack or suitcase), or a rope whose resistance is controlled by friction.

Runners choose their weight training both for general body strength and for specific running muscles. These basic exercises are often recommended for building your all-around strength:

Clean and press (plus related lifts). With the barbell on the floor, grasp the bar — palms down, knees slightly bent, shoulders hunched and back arched, arms straight down. The first movement is a dead lift in which you straighten your back by pulling your shoulders back and pushing your hips forward. Next, you "clean" the barbell until it is in front of your face, above your forearms. Next, you do the military press by pushing the barbell overhead until your arms are straight. You should add a shoulder shrug at the clean position and a toe raise at the end.

Lower the barbell with the reverse motions, at about the same speed. This is probably the best all-around conditioner. If you progress to heavy weights, you may endanger your spinal column; runners should limit themselves to their body weight.

Abdominal curl. This is a sit-up, but with your knees bent and your back arched to make your abdominal muscles work instead of your hip flexors. Anchor your feet under something heavy. As you become stronger, hold a weight behind your neck. Twist your body as you rise, touching a knee with the opposite elbow.

Side bends. To add to your trunk strength, use a heavy dumbbell. Let it hang freely from one arm. Bend sideways as far as you can, then bend to the other side. After several repetitions, switch hands.

Arm strengtheners. Ron Clarke used a wall pulley and made running motions with his arms. You can use dumbbells, too. For endurance, continue until your arms are tired.

The important leg exercises are:

Heel raise. Place a barbell across your shoulders and raise as high as you can on your toes. You can lengthen the distance of contraction and also give a welcome stretch to your Achilles tendon by elevating your toes on a block. A variation of this exercise is used by Soviet runners. They jog slowly with a heavier weight on their shoulders.

Naturally, they barely shuffle along, but this produces endurance, compared with the pure strength of the heel raise.

Knee raise. In this exercise, you simply raise your knee toward your chest against resistance from a weight attached to your foot in an iron boot. (Or you can balance a weighted sack on your knee, or lift against a wall pulley or friction rope.)

Leg press. Any number of movements will strengthen the power of your leg drive toward the track. The most common is the squat (half of a deep-knee bend with a heavy weight across your shoulders). Better for your spine is the inverted leg press (lie down and push up against a machine). A bicycle movement against the resistance of a friction rope will accomplish the same strengthening.

Several varieties of movements can be made while carrying a weight on your shoulders: Step Ups or Reverse Step Ups (onto a bench or block); Bouncing Split Squats (jump to a position with one bent knee forward and the other leg extended to the rear, then jump up and reverse your legs); Single Leg Jump Squat (put one foot on a block and spring as high as you can); Skip Running (alternate legs, leaping for height on each skip).

Leg extension. Sit on a bench, hook your ankles under a padded barbell (or weighted iron boots), and lift your feet until your legs are straight.

Leg curl. Lie on your stomach on a bench and lift your heels toward your buttocks against resistance. If you do not have use of an expensive machine for this lift, you can use iron boots while standing.

Certain lifts are of no value or are harmful to runners. Even heavy squats are not advisable because of the possibility of knee injuries.

Along with the question of *which* exercises to use, you must consider the question of *how much* of each one you should do.

John Jesse recommends three times a week as the proper amount of weight training during your off season, then twice a week. He recommends no increase in the weights you lift during your competitive season. Ward, who believes in great strength, recommends spreading your lifting over the week by doing only one or two exercises a day. Others advise only one lifting session per week during your season of competition.

"How much strength is required by an athlete for championship performance in his event?" asks Jesse. "Science or the coach cannot specifically answer this question, other than to say no sport in itself develops the level of strength required to meet and overcome the emergency situations that arise in competition."[59]

Somewhere between not enough strength and too much lies the optimum amount. A doubling of your strength (100 percent increase) must certainly help, but, of course, it depends upon how strong you are to begin with. An increase of 400 percent seems like too much for distance runners. When you have doubled your strength it may not harm you to let it increase still further, especially if you run the 800 meters. It is probably better to hold your new strength by continuing with the same weights. At the same time, you can increase the repetitions for added endurance.

Another element you should consider in limiting your weight training is the total amount of energy you spend. Your psychological and adaptive energy is limited, and you do not want to cut down on your running efforts because of excess weightlifting.

One of the advantages of weightlifting is that you can measure your work. The method of progressive gains in strength recommended most often requires you to lift a weight that you can repeat at least five times but not 10.

If you are trying to gain the maximum possible amount of strength, you continue to add weights as you learn to handle them. But if you are a runner, using weight training to improve your running, you must obviously draw the line somewhere. It would seem logical that double strength (twice the amount you can develop by running alone) has enough safety margin in both directions. If added repetitions, for endurance training, adds to your strength, it will not be enough to harm you.

Travers advises: "The optimum period of work for any muscle group is to the point of muscle fatigue." He suggests the following program for general fitness training:

"The weight schedule is made up of simple exercises in which each part of the body is exercised in turn. . . The 10 rep weight is that weight with which the exercise can just be completed 10 times and no more. These weights are recorded and are used in subsequent training sessions. At the first session each exercise is performed 10 times. At each subsequent session an attempt is made to add one repetition to each exercise and the circuit is always completed once only . . . When the number of repetitions for each exercise has increased to 20, the 10 rep/max is remeasured and the whole process is started again. Thus we increase the repetition from 10 to 20 against a given load, then increase the load and repeat the increase from 10 to 20 again."[132]

You should be careful not to do this indefinitely. When your 10 rep/max weight has doubled from your starting weight, you should consider avoiding further increase in strength. Somebody must put a limit on your increase, whether scientifically or not.

In addition to thinking about the kind and amount of weight training you do, you must remember certain rules. Travers warns: "Any athlete who is starting to use weights for the first time is well advised to seek the aid of a qualified weight-training coach or at least someone who has knowledge of the techniques and skills involved. There are risks in weight training, but they are not sufficient to offset the benefits which it brings provided that these simple safety precautions are observed; however, it is criminal carelessness to invite injury by disregarding these common sense measures."[132]

He lists these safety measures:

• Lift correctly, with a straight back, keeping the weight close to your body.

• Avoid a slippery floor or grip.

• Make sure weights are securely fastened.

• Have someone with you when lifting heavy weights.

• Warm up with lighter weights for 20 minutes.

Costes warns against tightening up: "Caution must be practiced when working with weights. For every weight exercise, immediately do a counter-stretching exercise and a 'shaking out.' This prevents that tight feeling, which restricts smooth, relaxed running. The more time a runner spends in weight training, the more he should devote to counter-stretching and shaking out."

Every time you tighten a muscle in weight training, follow it by stretching the same muscle.

Costes also advises weight training before your running workout, avoiding hard weight training and hard running on the same day, and a reduction in lifting, if a feeling of lightness persists while running.

The latest development in strength training is electrical stimulation. Believe it or not, the Soviets have been using electricity to improve strength since 1968, and their Olympic champions have benefited. They claim strength gains up to 50 percent in 20 days, all without the strain of weight training![42]

The weaker you are to begin with, the more you need weight training. The shorter your race, the more you need added strength. If you run the steeplechase or cross-country, you need extra strength. Properly acquired, extra strength will not harm your running, and it may surprise you with added speed and endurance.

5

Speed Training

Speed helps you at all distances, but the question of what is speed and what is endurance is like the question of which came first, the chicken or the egg.

For example, if you cannot run a 440 faster than 60 seconds, no amount of endurance will enable you to run a mile under four minutes. On the other hand, if you can run 100 meters in 10-flat your great speed is useless in a 10,000-meter race unless you develop adequate endurance.

To complicate the question still further, speed seems to complement endurance and vice versa. Thus, a 46-flat 400-meter runner needs less endurance to run an 800 in 1:49 than does a 49-flat man. And a trained miler can often run a 400 as fast as a far speedier sprinter who has not trained for endurance.

Speed is important, but the longer your race the less you need speed. If, after you are in good condition, you cannot run a 200 faster than 26 seconds, you cannot hope to be a great middle-distance runner.

To understand speed we must differentiate between three kinds of running speed:

1) Sprinting. This means competition in the 100 and 200, not part of this book.

2) Finishing kick. This is a type of speed, but it also involves other factors. It is discussed elsewhere in this book.

3) Effective speed. You cannot use your full speed in races longer than a sprint, but you can use some of it. If you are one second faster at 100 meters, it is equal to seven minutes in a marathon.

At any distance, greater speed means you can run easier at that pace, and so your endurance is taxed less. This means, in effect, your endurance is increased. If you can, for example, improve your race pace by one-tenth of a second for each 100 meters with no increase in effort, your time for 5000 meters will be five seconds faster. Therefore, to run your best, no matter what your distance, you need to develop your speed.

Sprinters are born with a higher percentage of fast-twitch muscle fibers and fast reaction times, but they need hard training to reach their top speeds. So do you.

To increase your speed it may help to begin by thinking about it. Pure running speed is simply your leg speed multiplied by your stride length. For example, if you take five steps per second and each is two meters long, you cover 10 meters in one second. You could run at the same speed with only four and one half strides per second, if your stride measured 2.22 meters.

Anything that increases either your stride length or leg speed without a corresponding sacrifice in the other will make you run faster. You can increase your speed by using any or all of these five methods:

1. Speedwork. You can improve your speed simply by running fast in training. That is how most sprinters trained until recent years. A few weeks of sharpening with speedwork before your competitive season will work magic on your distance times. But other speed work will help you improve even more.

2. Strength. Stronger running muscles will lengthen your stride without extra energy, and it can also quicken your stride. (This was discussed in the previous chapter.)

Senior English coach Frank Horwill promises: "Six months of once-a-week sprinting, weight training twice a week, and you'll knock seconds off your 400 time."

3. Flexibility. Tightness in your muscles and joints can shorten your stride as well as slow it. Unfortunately, distance running causes tightness, and so does strength training.

You should do flexibility exercises regularly to maintain looseness in your running. Several times a day may be beneficial, depending on how stiff you are.

Many exercises promote flexibility. Yoga will help, but if you are short of time do those that stretch the back of your legs and torso. That is where runners need help.

You can use your favorite exercises, but here are two to stretch your tight muscles from your heels to your waist:

• Calf stretch. Thrust one leg back and force your heel toward the floor. Straighten your leg and push until you feel a stretching sensation. This should stretch both your calf muscles and your Achilles tendon. Hold for a few seconds.

• Hamstring stretch. You can stretch your hamstring muscles in many ways. Most common is "touching your toes," but this can aggravate lower-back problems. You can sit on the floor and do the same stretch. You can stand with one leg on a table and hold your stretch for a few seconds at a time. Or you can do backovers, which stretch your lower back muscles, as well as your hamstrings.

You should stretch each group of muscles a total of a minute, before and after running or weight training. Add more stretching if you feel stiff.

4. Decreased Resistance Running. If you use something that allows your legs to move faster than you can move them while sprinting, you can increase your leg speed. Three methods have proven effective:

• Treadmill running can force your legs to move faster than you are capable of moving them during normal sprinting. This is because of lack of wind resistance and the need for a strong push-off. Treadmills are complicated and expensive equipment.

• Downhill running. If you sprint downhill, your legs will move faster than is possible on the level. Experiments, particularly in Europe, have proved your leg speed can be increased in this way. The ideal slope was found to be 2.6 degrees. The best results are attained if you alternate downhill running with level running.

• Towing. Al Lawrence of Australia recommends the tow method, in which you hang onto a tow bar behind an automobile. Lawrence tried it in 1956 when he hoped to make the Olympic team. He ran at speeds as fast as 17.5 for a 220 and 1:10 for 660 yards. After six weeks, he lowered the Australian record for 10,000 meters to 29:50 and in another two months he ran 29:20. Six weeks later, he ran 28:53.6 and took home the Olympic bronze medal. Lawrence credits Cecil Nensley with developing other runners by using this method.

Charles Sandwick reported cases of sprinters who improved their average 100-yard times from 10.5 to 9.9 in five weeks of towing.[117]

5. Form. There is another aspect of distance running that must be considered as speed. That aspect is running efficiency. The more efficiently you use your available energy, the faster you will run. If you learn correct running form, it is possible for an opponent to have faster sprint speed than you, while you have a more efficient running form that makes you faster.

You will run thousands of miles in training. Your main concentration during most of those miles should be on developing the most efficient running form possible.

Before you start concentrating, you should understand some of the principles involved:

Foot Placement. There is more controversy over this subject than most others. Arguments rage as to which of three methods of foot placement is correct: ball first, heel first, or flat-footed. The answer is none of these. In the correct foot placement, the side of your foot touches first.

Which part of the side of your foot depends upon your shoe and your pace. A sprint shoe with long spikes makes it almost impossible to touch anything but the ball or your little toe first. Those road running shoes with heels make it almost necessary to touch the side of your heel first. But in general, at faster speeds you touch farther forward on your foot.

In distance running, experts agree that you rest your full weight on your flat foot during each stride. They also agree that your foot does not touch very far ahead of your center of gravity in distance running. If both are true, then it is obvious that the time between the moment when part of your foot touches and the time when your foot is flat on the ground is fractions of a second.

Therefore, it would seem to make little difference which part of the edge of your foot touches first. The important consideration is that you do not bear your weight on your toes and thus tire your calves unnecessarily, and that you do not land on your heel with your toes lifted and thus jar your body.

You will hear all kinds of descriptions of the footplant, but Toni Nett of Germany filmed it to find out exactly what runners do. Nett confirmed that the longer the distance of the race, the farther back was the point of contact. He wrote:

"At all distances beyond 1500 meters, up to the marathon, a first contacting of the ground with the outside edge at the arch between the heel and the metatarsus is confirmed. . . Further, it was interesting that many distance runners. . . upon being questioned, thought they ran on the ball of the foot while the infallible camera eye quite clearly refuted them."[92]

Austrailia's Lawrence wrote: "While in Canada for the British Empire Games in 1954 I watched Roger Bannister, John Landy, Chris Chataway and Jim Peters, the marathon runner. All used the ball-heel-ball method of footplant. That made up my mind. I changed to the natural ball, heel, ball footplant, and the improvement in my times and racing performances were phenomenal."[75]

It is possible that most runners believe they are using the ball-heel-ball method. And it is possible that some actually do, although few have ever landed as high on their toes as Van Nelson.

Percy Cerutty's description of the proper foot plant, however, agrees with Toni Nett:

"It is now known that the foot does not land as was hitherto thought. The slow-motion camera has altered all that. No more is the tensed leg controlled to a ball of foot landing, nor do we rock-over and so on.

"The camera shows us that the foot approaches the ground with toes cocked up as if it was to be a heel landing. Yet at speed it isn't. Nor is it a ball-of-the-foot landing. In very slow motion it can be viewed as a slow slither with a caressing movement from the outside of the whole foot to the inside, embodying a clampdown movement much as we use to stamp on a coin rolling to the gutter — a very quick movement."[21]

This quick movement must become second nature and unconscious, but when you are first learning to run properly you must get the feel of it. You must avoid striving artificially to use some other footplant. This natural way uses the least energy.

Lydiard advises "a nearly flat foot because it is an easier, more natural action for covering long distances."[77]

The ball-heel-ball footplant is natural for middle-distance speeds. Anything else is slower. You can get the feel of it quickly by walking barefoot. Instead of jarring down on your heels or remaining awkwardly on tip-toe, let the front side of your foot touch first, then put all your weight on your flat foot as you lift your other foot. Herb Elliott demonstrated this form beautifully and called it the "classic" way of walking.

You must feel the naturalness of this method before you can run properly, and so this is the basis of correct form. A long-distance runner can run with his heel touching first or almost flat-footed, but you will do better at middle distances by practicing ball-heel-ball even while you are putting in your long mileage.

Rear Leg Lift. Emil Zatopek ran with almost no rear leg lift, and many other runners have attempted to do the same so as to avoid excess movement. John T. Powell comments on this:

"Should it matter how high the heel flicks up behind? No! We are interested in speed, and a short lever (radius) travels faster than a long one. With the lower leg out of the way, the thigh can swing through faster for the next stride. The faster the athlete, the higher will rise the heel behind. The heel's rise is thus proportional to the force exerted and is a reaction to the power used."[100]

Thus, you must not make an effort to hold your heel down. It requires extra energy for you to do so!

Length of Stride. This is the most critical part of your distance running form, and the part you can do the most about.

Sprinters take the longest strides, but they are not concerned with saving energy. Zatopek's stride in a 5000-meter race was measured at 5 feet 11 inches; Popov, the marathoner, had a stride of only 5 feet 3 inches.

Dr. Roskamm wrote: "Consideration must, of course, be given to the physical height of the athlete. Only Nurmi's length of stride in his 1500-meter runs was found to have been too great in relation to his speed; his stride in these being from 7 feet 5 inches to 7 feet 7 inches, while a length of from 6 feet 3 inches to 6 feet 11 inches would have been more advantageous for his pace. Thus, while his style was elegant, it was uneconomical. The experiments have shown that the long stride at slow speed can be uneconomical. Munchinger proves this with his findings that the center of gravity in the moment of the forward 'jump' is being lifted too sharply, and that the necessary hip and shoulder counterthrust consumes too much energy."[111]

Strangely enough, that simple fact of physics was ignored by runners and coaches for many years. As late as 1949 an article[86] tried to point this out to Americans, but another article in late 1952[87] expressed disappointment over the lack of progress.

One dramatic example of the advantage of a short stride took place in August 1952. Charlie Capozzoli made the U.S. Olympic team with his best 5000-meter time of 14:43.9. At Helsinki he ran 14:39.0 while failing to qualify. Two weeks later he ran in London against runners who placed in the Olympics. He had been practicing a short, economical stride, but he did not have the courage to use it in the Olympics. At London, his change of form was startling, and he won the three-mile race against Pirie and the others in national-record time of 13:51.8, about 20 seconds faster than his previous best.

Some middle-distance runners take much longer strides than others at the same speed. You do not have this option in sprinting, where you must use long and fast strides, nor in long-distance running, where you cannot continue with a long stride. In the 800, especially, runners with long, loping strides have been successful. Notable among these exceptions were John Woodruff, Arnie Sowell, Mal Whitfield and Don Bowden.

The long, slow stride is usually inefficient. It requires extra energy to lift your body higher into the air. Your speed slows while you are in the air and you need an extra push to accelerate again. And your extended foot hits the track too far in front of your center of gravity, acting as a brake before your body can move to a position over your foot.

And yet there seems to be more latitude in middle-distance running. Stride lengths might vary by as much as a foot for men of the same height.

Interval workouts are the diet of runners who want to improve their speed. University of Oregon coach Bill Dellinger uses a stopwatch in an interval session that includes Al Salazar, Rudy Chapa and Bill McChesney, circa 1978.

In choosing your stride length for the middle distances, you should start with your natural stride. If you are a miler who sometimes runs 5000s, and your natural stride is short, you might leave it alone except for *allowing* it to lengthen when you run faster.

If you are an 800 person who also runs 400s, and your natural stride is long, you are safe. But if your natural stride is short, you should experiment with lengthening it. The miler who runs longer races should try to shorten a long stride. In each case, you should tend toward medium length. An extreme in either direction should be modified.

At the same time you are making these gross changes in form, you should be working toward a longer stride of the right type. Assuming you have modified your stride to the right length, you should have as your goal the addition of an inch or two to your stride without changing anything else. (See strength training.)

Developing the proper stride length for each of your various speeds is probably the most complicated of all the things you must learn. It calls for much thought and concentration.

Body Angle. The angle of your lean while running is of little importance as long as it is natural to you and is nearly upright. You must lean when you accelerate, but make no conscious effort otherwise.

Posture *is* important. Dr. Donald B. Slocum, clinical professor of orthopedic surgery at the University of Oregon, was quoted as saying, "A study of some excellent runners. . . has demonstrated that the erect trunk posture with a flat back in mid-support is consistent with good running performance. . . if they hold their backs straight instead of plunging after their heads in the traditional pose favored by coaches for decades."[43]

It is important that you hold your head and chest high, so as to make full breathing easier.

Arms. The purpose of your arm action is to balance your leg action. If you allow your arms to swing naturally, without forcing them into extra motion, you probably have good arm action.

You should force no change unless your arms are causing your shoulders to swing or they are held too close in front so that they cramp your chest position and prevent full breathing. The angle made at your elbow should be about 90 degrees, usually a little less.

In faster running, your arm angle often changes during each stride. Sprinters tend to increase the angle, toward a straighter arm, when the hand goes down. Then the angle decreases on the upswing. Herb Elliott's action was exactly opposite, which gave the effect of moving his hands almost parallel to the track.

The late Percy Cerutty believed your arms lead your legs. Certainly, most coaches agree that you should use your arms to lead during an all-out sprint. Otherwise, the most important point to watch in all other running is your energy output. Do not waste energy on your arm swing.

Leg Drive. An important aspect of distance running form is your method of applying power to your stride. First, there is no possibility of pulling from in front of your center of gravity. When your full weight is on your flattened foot, your foot should be under your hip. You cannot reach out and pull yourself forward.

All the force that drives you forward is applied behind your center of gravity. In sprinting, which is mechanically efficient but a waste of energy, you make a powerful push off your toes as you leave the ground. But the slower you run, the less push you need. A strong push would send you farther forward and higher in the air, an obviously inefficient method. Keep your momentum going with a minimum of lift.

Total Action. You should develop a feeling for the proper action in distance running form. Gerry Lindgren's legs moved almost as fast as a sprinter's. He wasted less energy with his fast leg action than most other runners.

Consider a duck flying all day at a fast speed. Its wings beat at a furious pace, and yet they never seem to tire. The speed of movement is much less a factor in tiring than the strength of movement. Thus, one long stride of eight feet takes much more strength than two four-foot strides.

In addition to spending much more energy lifting your body high enough for a long stride, you lose energy at the end of the stride. If your foot comes down in front of you, your leg has a braking action, which slows your speed. Therefore, you should use the shorter, natural stride because it requires the least possible energy to maintain your speed. As you increase your speed, your stride lengthens.

Your stride must be "light and easy." Think of your legs as wheels instead of two objects moving back and forth. Each foot goes up in the rear, swings forward with no effort below your knee, and starts moving backward before it touches the track. You land on it below your center of gravity and move over it with almost no feeling of a push-off.

When you watch another runner in action, you can usually see some wasted motion. His knees lift too high, or his stride is too long, or he bounds too high, or his feet pound, or his shoulders swing. You cannot see yourself run, although a coach can. Also, you might make use of video tapes of yourself; nevertheless, you can *feel* your total running action.

Whenever you run at a speed near your race pace, you should "feel" for any wasted motion. If you land too hard, or feel jerky, or wobble, or stay in the air too long, or feel any tension or effort in your legs, you should try to correct it. Next to developing your endurance, this is the most important part of your training.

Once you have smoothed out your running form, you need little work on it, but you must learn to hold that form when you are tired. The more fatigued you are in a race, the more important it is to hold your form. You can accomplish this by first learning proper form, and then by practicing it whenever you run.

You should not sharpen your speed with sprinting and decreased resistance running until after you are in excellent condition, but you should maintain flexibility and work on an efficient form year around.

Marty Liquori says, "I do some speed work all year. . . I never go out and train a week straight without going on the track. . . at least one or two days a week."

6

Combining Speed with Endurance

One of the most amazing feats of nature is the amount of work your body can do anaerobically (without oxygen). Sprinters often run 100 meters without taking a breath. Even if they do breathe, none of that oxygen reaches the muscles in time to be used. Oxygen must be inside you for 40 seconds before it can be used for energy.

When you run faster than the aerobic threshold, part of your energy is anaerobic. This source of energy is not completely understood, but it is important enough to your running to be worth studying:

1) The first energy you use is your immediate store of ATP (adenosine triphosphate). The breaking of these high-energy bonds enables you to act instantly, without waiting for more complicated chemical processes. Your supply of ATP lasts only part of a second and you cannot continue your movement unless more ATP is synthesized.

2) Fortunately, you have a supply of CP (creatine phosphate) in your muscle cells. This CP transfers its phosphate to ADP and you have ATP again. Your muscles have enough CP stored to keep you going for several seconds.

These two sources of energy are anaerobic, but they are not the kind you are studying. They furnish energy without forming lactic acid and so this anaerobic method is called alactacid. You can start running by using only alactacid energy, but in only a few seconds you must resynthesize ATP in some other way.

3) Inside your muscle cells you have a substance much like the hemoglobin in your blood, myoglobin, which can carry oxygen. This oxygen is the first to be used to make more ATP. When that is used — in a few seconds — you begin to use oxygen that was in your blood before you started running. This is followed by oxygen that was in your lungs before you started running.

Thus, it is impossible to make an exact measurement of your energy from lactic acid, because if you started running without breathing, part of your energy would come from oxygen stored in your body and part of your anaerobic energy would be alactacid.

As you continue to run, having used up all of the above emergency sources of energy, your main sources depend upon how fast you are running.

4) Your principle method of rebuilding ATP is the aerobic way (oxidative phosphorylation). Glucose goes through six chemical changes during glycolysis in your muscle cells and it becomes pyruvic acid. If you are not running too fast, this pyruvic acid goes into a series of reactions called the Krebs Cycle (also: citric acid cycle or tricarboxylic acid cycle). This is the main pathway where fresh oxygen enters biological oxidation for the first time to oxidize carbohydrates, fats and proteins. Water and carbon dioxide are thrown off, and about 90 percent of all your ATP is produced here in the cytoplasm of your cells.

Most of the movements you make — from breathing to easy walking — require no more energy than this aerobic kind. You go on breathing for a lifetime without requiring anaerobic energy to move your ribs and diaphragm. But when your movements require more energy than you can supply from the oxygen you breathe — as happens in all middle-distance running — you must find still another source of energy.

5) Your final method of resynthesizing ATP is through production of lactic acid. When your speed crosses the border into anaerobic running, some of your pyruvic acid must be changed to lactic acid to furnish the extra ATP you need. (This is a simple chemical step in which pyruvic acid loses two hydrogen atoms.) Thus, the sum total of energy you use during a run is divided into three main parts:

• Your stored, "instant" energy. This is partly from stored oxygen and partly from anaerobic energy, which does not result in lactic acid production. The best scientific guess[79] is that this furnishes you with about 0.14 kilocalories of energy per kilogram of body weight. That is enough energy to run 150 yards.

• Your aerobic energy. In this "steady state," a super runner with his glycogen supply intact can produce about 0.37 kcal/kg, enough energy to run 400 yards per minute.

• Your lactacid energy. Roddfo Margaria[79] gives the total amount of lactacid energy available as about 0.22 kcal/kg, enough energy to run almost 240 yards. But this figure is highly debatable.

Unfortunately, science has not yet been able to measure this exactly. It is unfortunate, because if you had such measurements you could decide exactly how to train.

Probably the easiest way to demonstrate that your immediately available anaerobic energy does not total 0.14 kcal/kg from alactacid sources, plus 0.22 from lactacid sources, is to try to run 150 yards, plus 240 yards — a total of 390 yards — without breathing — at any pace you choose.

There are many reasons why it has been impossible, to date, to measure man's lactacid capacity. For half a century, the concept of "oxygen debt" has been examined, and physiologists assumed it was a simple measurement — the difference between your resting oxygen consumption and the amount you use after you stop running. This extra oxygen you consume is used for several purposes, in addition to repaying borrowed lactacid energy:

• Your basal oxygen consumption continues no matter what your activity. Your brain and your non-running muscles need oxygen to stay alive. This totals about four milliliters of oxygen per kilogram of body weight per minute.

• Hard exercise increases your basal consumption about two-fold.[80] This extra consumption continues for hours after a hard run.

• Any movements you make during recovery require oxygen.

• Your stores of oxygen are depleted when you finish. About eight milliliters of oxygen per kilogram of weight goes to replenish your depleted blood and the myoglobin of your cells.[79]

• Some oxygen must be used to resynthesize your ATP and CP before you can begin to repay your debt. This is calculated to be about 20 ml/kg.[79] This debt is paid rapidly, at a rate of 50 percent in about half a minute.[80]

• You must pay interest on your debt. This interest may be as high as 100 percent. This interest is necessary because energy is needed for the process of glycogenesis, wherein your lactic acid is changed back to glycogen. This is a relatively slow process.

• Finally, you must repay, with oxygen, every calorie of energy you borrowed. Since it is impossible to measure all the other oxygen, it is impossible to measure the direct repayment for lactacid energy.

And yet, to learn how to train your lactacid mechanism to its capacity, you should have some idea of the size of that capacity.

One way to determine your lactacid capacity is through an examination of the lactic acid in your blood after exercise. Lactic acid is the end product thrown off from pyruvic acid while energy is produced anaerobically by glycolysis. Production starts when you are running at about two-thirds of your maximum aerobic capacity. You use the ATP for energy and the lactic acid accumulates. It begins to diffuse from your cells into your blood.

Physiologists can measure the amount of lactic acid in your blood. Margaria's figures[80] show about three milligrams of lactic acid per 100 milliliters of blood is equal to 1.0 ml/kg. This gives a rough idea of the amount of lactacid energy you have expended, but there are at least two serious sources of error:

• Lactic acid diffuses into your blood stream for five to eight minutes after you stop running.[80] To find your highest lactic acid level a physiologist must take blood samples for at least eight minutes. Usually only one sample is taken; if it is not taken at your highest level, then your highest level is unknown.

• Since this indicates that lactic acid does not diffuse into your blood at the same rate it is produced, no accurate measurement of your lactacid energy is possible. Furthermore, lactic acid is produced for several seconds after exercise ceases.[80]

• Another discrepancy is that lactic acid leaves your blood continuously, even while you are exercising.[113] Some of it goes to resting muscles where it is oxidized to carbon dioxide and water. Some is used by your heart and other organs. About half of it is converted to glycogen in your liver and viscera.[113] The rest is converted to glycogen in the cortex of your kidneys.

• This removal of lactic acid apparently takes place only when it reaches a certain level in your blood. People have a little lactic acid in their blood at all times, usually around 10 to 15 mg/100 ml — about 8 percent of their maximum capacity. Thus, the lower levels of blood lactates cannot be precisely accurate for measuring anaerobic energy.

Certain conclusions can be made from still other evidence — the empirical results of actual runners. For example, most runners who are in condition can only maintain 85 to 90 percent of their speed for 400 meters, even though they can maintain close to 100 percent for about 300 meters. This evidence that your anaerobic power will not last through 400 meters places a very real limit on that power.

The most important remaining question concerning anaerobic training: How much does one runner's lactacid power vary from another's?

If lactacid power *does* vary, and if it can be measured, then by examining training methods you will learn which methods produce the greatest power.

Unfortunately, the production of lactic acid is a chemical reaction, not subject to training, and so pyruvic acid changes to lactic acid and produces ATP at the same rate, whether you are trained or not. Normal resting blood lactate is about 10 milligrams per 100 milliliters of blood. Almost everybody, trained or untrained, shows the same maximum level of lactic acid in his blood — about 150 milligrams per 100 milliliters of blood.

Whatever improvement is made in your lactacid power by training, it is not a change in your chemistry. It could well be connected with the glycogen content of your muscles, as Margaria[79] states. But if it is the same increase in glycogen you get from long-distance running, then the best training for the lactacid power needed in the 400 is long runs of 20 miles or more!

There is very little difference in the lactacid capacity of various runners. For most trained men, a best time in the 400 is a direct function of basic speed. If you are one second faster at 100 meters, you will be four seconds faster at 400 meters.

All this indicates that there is relatively little difference between middle-distance runners in their lactacid power. And this difference is too small to measure, given the inexact measuring tools available. At most, this difference seems to be no more than 1.0 ml/kg.

This sameness of lactacid power in all middle-distance runners leads to a startling observation: In spite of extreme variations in training methods, there is little difference in results.

This fact relieves you of the single most onerous burden carried by middle-distance runners: Unlimited punishment does not result in unlimited improvement.

Experienced and perceptive runners and coaches know this. Many of the hardest-training runners have failed miserably in competition.

Marty Liquori's comments are worth pondering: He said, "When Americans say, 'I went on the track' they usually go on the track and work out until they can't do another thing." And: "The majority of the serious runners in this country are overtrained."

Therefore, there are four good reasons for not punishing yourself with the maximum amount of all-out training:

• You can reach your maximum lactacid power without extreme training. Lasse Viren, the strongest finisher in distance running history, trains on the track only three times a year. He considers himself fortunate that he was ignorant of interval training for years.

• Going deep into oxygen debt is unpleasant. At best it takes much of the joy out of your sport. At worst, it will cause you to give up racing much sooner.

O. Karikosk of Estonia made an extensive study of middle-distance training, and he warns us about anaerobic training. He concludes, "Record performances in the junior ranks make future successes of young distance runners extremely doubtful."[63]

• Even more important, when you go deep into oxygen debt you cannot continue for long. This prevents you from doing the volume of training necessary to improve your other qualities. You cannot improve your aerobic capacity if your workout is limited to six 300s.

Lydiard says, "When you do anaerobic work, your oxygen uptake level starts coming down. The secret of training is to do the necessary anaerobic-type work without losing your conditioning."[50]

• The greatest danger of excess anaerobic training is that this extreme stress harms your body. It leads to failing adaptation. Then you are unable to run as well in training or in races.

Hans Selye wrote about excess stress: "Experiments on animals have clearly shown that each exposure leaves an indelible scar, in that it uses up reserves of adaptability which cannot be replaced. . . It is the restoration of superficial adaptation energy from the deep reserves that tricks us into believing that the loss has been made good. Actually, it has only been covered from reserves — and at the cost of depleting reserves."[122]

How do you recognize the right amount of anaerobic training?

You can recognize the upper limits when you detect any failing adaptation to stress. Even your failure to recover within a day should make you wary.

It is more difficult to recognize the minimum amount of anaerobic work necessary to reach your capacity. The most useful starting point in this examination is to begin with Bob Deines, America's best at 50 miles in 1970, who did no interval training and almost no fast training. Using calculations based on the Energy Formula, Deines' lactacid capacity is seen to be at least 90 percent of the maximum possible to any runner. And Ron Clarke, who did little interval training, had a calculated lactacid capacity of about 95 percent of the maximum.

This must be discouraging to those runners who have punished themselves severely for years in an attempt to build greater lactacid power. Part of the explanation is fairly simple:

Certain pathways of aerobic metabolism are identical or helpful to anaerobic metabolism. All of the steps from muscle glycogen to pyruvic acid are the same no matter how fast you run. Your speed affects only pyruvic acid, converting some of it to lactic acid to obtain energy your aerobic system fails to provide. Therefore, even slow running trains the first part of your metabolism, and it also increases your supply of glycogen. You cannot run anaerobically without glycogen.

It is estimated that varied borderline running, plus a season of middle-distance racing, would raise your lactacid capacity to 98 percent of the possible maximum.

That missing 2 percent, however, is important to a middle-distance runner. It could make about one second difference in your 800 time.

It is impossible to know exactly how to train for that last 2 percent. To a runner who wants to improve right down to the last tenth of a second, there is no other answer than to do a little extra anaerobic training to be certain. If this extra training is done early enough so that you can recover in time for important races, no physical harm should result from it.

There is so little difference between aerobically trained runners and anaerobically trained, and so little is known scientifically, that this may very well be the case. It is quite possible that the difference is *not* improved lactacid power, but rather a combination of three things:

• Greater speed from so much fast training. This means the ability to use a speed closer to your maximum speed with more skill and efficiency.

• Greater strength from running faster than your race pace over and over again.

• Greater capillarization of "fringe muscles" used only in what amounts to resistance running.

If this hypothesis is true, then the same results can be accomplished by using methods already mentioned, without the unpleasantness of repeated all-out running. In fact, if this hypothesis is true, then not even one short four- to six-week period need be devoted to anaerobic training during the year. Your lactacid power could be fully developed through extensive aerobic training and speed training, plus special exercises for strength and additional capillaries. This may explain why so many varied training programs have worked reasonably well.

There remains an empirical method of examining this problem. Roughly, this is to note how many times successful runners go deep into oxygen debt during training. This cannot be anything like a scientific study because the problem contains too many variables and too many unknowns instead of exact measurements, but a rough consideration may be of value.

The variables consist mainly of the number of times you go into oxygen debt and how far into debt you go. A thorough study would record the percentage of your maximum debt used, from 1 percent to 100 percent, for each run. The study would show the number of times you went into debt for each workout, number of workouts per day, week, and month, and the seasons of the year all this took place.

Instead of measuring the exact percentage of oxygen debt, a guess can be made and each workout can be scored on one of the following levels:

0 — No lactic acid (LA) produced in the workout. (Long, slow run.)

1 — Little LA produced once in a workout. (Borderline.)

2 — Little LA produced repeatedly in one workout. (Varied borderline running, or 100s at your race pace.)

3 — Moderate LA (about 25 percent of maximum) produced once in a workout. (Varied borderline, or one 400 faster than race pace.)

4 — Moderate LA produced repeatedly in one workout. (Several 200s at your race pace, with adequate rest.)

5 — Medium LA (about 50 percent of maximum) produced once. (First half of your race.)

6 — Medium LA produced repeatedly in one workout. (Race-pace fartlek, maintaining your LA level at about the 5 level.)

7 — Much LA (about 75 percent of maximum) produced once. (Equivalent to the first three-quarters of your mile pace.)

8 — Much LA produced repeatedly in one workout. (Hard race-pace fartlek, or any fast intervals with recovery periods geared to allow only a little rest.)

9 — Near-maximum LA (almost 100 percent) produced once. (A race or hard time-trial, or hard intervals.)

10 — Near-maximum LA produced repeatedly in one workout. (Any interval or repetition workout that is continued after you reach near-maximum oxygen debt.)

It is all but impossible to analyze a runner's lactic acid production from his training schedule. At best, it is a guess, for this degree of oxygen indebtedness is not reported. Apparently, few people consider it important. This may be because so much training is done without a specific purpose in mind.

If any sense is ever to be made of training methods, all comparisons must be based upon the amount of lactic acid formed. The secret of training is to know your lactacid.

If your specific purpose is to go into oxygen debt so as to increase your anaerobic capacity, it is difficult to make comparisons with well-known runners, even through their workouts are recorded by Fred Wilt in *How They Train* and *Track Technique*. That is because much of the following is no more than an approximation based on an estimation:

One way to compare anaerobic training would be to record how many times each year a runner trains at each level. The highest level of 10 is a harder workout than almost any race, and very few of the top-flight runners train that hard.

It is estimated that Herb Elliott may have reached the 10 level about 50 times in one year, and Roger Moens about 25. It is revealing to learn that this 10 level has been reached most often by runners who are completely unknown today.

The 9 level — a single run of the same intensity as a race — is seldom reached in training. John Walker says, "I find it impossible to run flat-out."

John Paul Jones, world-record miler in 1913, ran about 34 of these in a year, but the only modern runners who used the 9 level were unknowns. Lydiard's 10-week schedule leading up to the big race suggests three such runs instead of weekly races. Most runners reach this level 20 to 30 times a year, in races.

The 8 level is quite commonly reached by good runners. Gunnar Nielsen probably ran to this level 150 times a year, and Derek Ibbotson even more often. Tom Courtney's training program reached the 8 level about 60 times per year, never higher. On the other hand, Lydiard recommends about seven such workouts, all in the last 10 weeks, and Jurgen May may have run only a dozen in a year. Jim Ryun may have run more of these than any other top runner, but he reached his peak at the age of 20. Istvan Rozsavolgyi, one of Igloi's best, shows an estimated 17 workouts at the 10 level and a like number at the 8 level.

The 7 level is probably reached regularly by most good runners, because few people believe in training without becoming tired. This is only one run, at any distance, which raises your lactic acid level to about 75 percent of your capacity. This level might be reached by runners attempting to do varied borderline running, but if so, it reduces their mileage.

As a semi-educated guess, based on the unscientific evidence in this chapter, here is what you should do to raise your lactacid power to its maximum:

Steve Scott became the miler who broke Jim Ryun's 1967 American mile record of 3:51.1, which lasted a phenomenal 14 years. On July 11, 1981, on foreign soil, Scott covered a mile in 3:49.7. He has since lowered the American mark to 3:47.7. In the Bruce Jenner Mile, Scott edges Eamonn Coghlan for the victory.

• Apparently no training at the 9 or 10 level is necessary if you race many times a year.

• You will reach the 7 level so many times you will not need to plan for it.

• Therefore, only the 8 level should be used for specific lactacid training. Assuming you race 25 times a year, you need relatively few training sessions at the 8 level. To be certain of reaching your maximum as an 800-meter runner, you may need three a week for a month or so. Two a week should do for a 5000-meter runner, and only one for a marathoner. If, for any reason, you do little racing, you should increase the number of hard workouts.

Arthur Lydiard: "I estimated that if we used anaerobic training for four weeks before a big race, this developed your anaerobic capacity to its maximum. The East Germans refined this and extended this period to five weeks. . . You need an exercise physiologist to control anaerobic training."[50]

Steve Scott, best U.S. miler of 1977, ran at the 8 level two or three times a week during his competitive season. World record-holder John Walker splits his season into three: build-up, speed, and racing. He does no 8 level anaerobic training except during his speed phase. This includes many 7 level sessions but only twice a week at the 8 level.

Summary:

• There is a limit to your capacity to go into lactacid debt.

• It is easier to reach that capacity than many runners think.

7

The Energy Formula

Until the development of modern medical procedures in the last 40 years, determining how hard you trained was a matter of guesswork. Everyone pretty much knew that effort was directly proportional to energy consumed, but that was all. Runners had no way of comparing the caloric cost of a 20-mile run at 8:00 minute pace to a 10-mile run at 5:00 minute pace.

Gradually, though, scientists applied breakthroughs in technology to the medical realm. Machines were made that could measure how much oxygen was used for a given effort. Calorie burnoff became more understandable as machines that could measure the energy in food were produced. It would be a few more years before runners could put all of the knowledge to good use. Meanwhile, coaches were responsible for guiding the runner, who gauged his effort by how he felt. If he ran hard one day and felt tired the next, he would rest until he felt like putting in an equally hard effort some days later. Science has finally given us measurements, though, to put our subjective thoughts into an objective context.

With this in mind, the Energy Formula was developed. No such formula can be exact, and since this is only the initial concept, no claim for accuracy can be made. Science has not yet progressed that far, and each runner's time is not always equal to his potential. Nevertheless, this formula should prove useful.

Everyone recognizes that if two runners are equal in all other respects, the one with the most speed will run a faster 800 or 1500. Or, the one with greater endurance will be superior at the 1500. Such basic understanding can be portrayed in a simple nomogram. To use it, connect any two known times with a straight-edge and read potential times for other distances.

NOMOGRAM

Speed (m/sec)	400	800	1500	3000	5000	10,000
9.5	46.5				13:00	45
9.4	47				05	
	47.5			7:30	10	28:00
9.3		1:43			15	
	48	44		35	20	15
9.2	48.5	45	3:30	40	25	
		46	32		30	30
	49	47	34	45	35	
9.1		48	36		40	45
	49.5	49	38	50	45	
9.0	50	50	40	55	50	29:00
	50.5	51	42		55	
8.9		52	44	8:00	14:00	15
	51	53	46	05	05	
8.8	51.5	54	48	10	10	30
		55	50		15	
8.7	52	56	52	15	20	45
	52.5	57	54	20	25	
8.6	53	58	56		30	30:00
		59	58	25	35	
8.5	53.5	2:00	4:00	30	40	15
	54	01	02		45	
8.4			04	35	50	30
			06		55	
8.3				40		

Here is the Energy Formula:

$$T = S + AC + LA - GD$$

The symbol T stands for the time of your race. In order to make this formula workable, all your energies are converted to milliliters of oxygen per kilogram. To express time in ml/kg/min, Margaria's[81] famous calculation is used: energy cost equals 1.0 kcal/kg/kilometer.

Since a liter of oxygen consumed in your body is equal to about five kilocalories of energy, the following table equates time to oxygen consumption:

800 METERS

95.0 = 1:41.0	91.0 = 1:45.5	87.0 = 1:50.3
94.0 = 1:42.1	90.0 = 1:46.7	86.0 = 1:51.6
93.0 = 1:43.2	89.0 = 1:47.9	85.0 = 1:52.9
92.0 = 1:44.4	88.0 = 1:49.1	84.0 = 1:54.3

1500 MILE

85.0 = 3:31.8/3:47.3	78.0 = 3:50.8/4:07.7
84.0 = 3:34.2/3:50.0	77.0 = 3:53.8/4:10.9
83.0 = 3:36.9/3:52.8	76.0 = 3:56.8/4:14.2
82.0 = 3:39.5/3:55.6	75.0 = 4:00.0/4:17.6
81.0 = 3:42.2/3:58.5	74.0 = 4:03.2/4:21.1
80.0 = 3:45.0/4:01.5	73.0 = 4:06.6/4:24.6
79.0 = 3:47.9/4:04.5	72.0 = 4:10.0/4:28.3

5000 METERS

76.0 = 13:09.5	72.0 = 13:53.3	68.0 = 14:42.4
75.0 = 13:20.0	71.0 = 14:05.1	67.0 = 14:55.5
74.0 = 13:30.8	70.0 = 14:17.2	66.0 = 15:09.1
73.0 = 13:42.0	69.0 = 14:29.6	65.0 = 15:23.1

10,000 METERS

73.0 = 27:24.0	69.0 = 28:59.2	65.0 = 30:46.2
72.0 = 27:46.2	68.0 = 29:24.6	64.0 = 31:15.0
71.0 = 28:10.0	67.0 = 29:51.0	63.0 = 31:45.0
70.0 = 28:34.4	66.0 = 30:18.2	62.0 = 32:15.6

MARATHON

65.0 = 2:09:49.8	59.0 = 2:23:01.8	53.0 = 2:39:13.2
64.0 = 2:11:51.6	58.0 = 2:25:30.0	52.0 = 2:42:17.4
63.0 = 2:13:57.0	57.0 = 2:28:03.0	51.0 = 2:45:28.2
62.0 = 2:16:06.6	56.0 = 2:30:41.4	50.0 = 2:48:46.8
61.0 = 2:18:20.4	55.0 = 2:33:25.8	49.0 = 2:52:13.2
60.0 = 2:20:39.0	54.0 = 2:36:16.8	48.0 = 2:55:48.6

The symbol S in the formula stands for *speed*. Each runner has a maximum speed, which can be expressed in meters per second. For example, a 10-flat runner averages 10 meters per second. But if you take off one second for his standing start, his average is 11.11 meters per second. Unfortunately, hand timing and starting errors make 100-meter times inaccurate, and so a 200-meter time is more reliable. Times for 200 meters give a maximum speed of about 96 percent of 100-meter times.

Another way to determine your speed is by use of the nomogram, but this requires your optimum times for two distances. Thus, your speed rating is only approximate, but because speed is so important in determining your racing times, some rating must be used.

Working on the nomogram, it was found that speed of 8.90 meters per second serves well as a median, or "zero" speed rating. Anything faster than 8.90 is given a plus speed rating. For example, if you can run 9.1 meters per second, your speed rating would be + .20. If you can run only 8.7 meters per second at top speed, your speed rating is − .20.

The Energy Formula uses ml/kg/min, and so your speed rating must be changed from meters per second to ml/kg/min. This is done by finding the difference between your speed in the tables of velocity and 106.95 ml/kg/min, which equals 8.92 meters per second. The result is your speed factor, expressed in plus or minus milliliters per kilogram per minute.

Your first step is to find your top speed in meters per second. Use the nomogram and as many columns as possible from the following table. A single sprint time is apt to give you a false impression of your speed.

TO FIND YOUR FULL SPEED:

meters/second	100 yards	100 meters	200, curve (5% added)
11.0	9.31	10.09	20.14
10.8	9.47	10.26	20.50
10.6	9.63	10.43	20.86
10.5	9.71	10.52	21.05
10.4	9.79	10.62	21.24
10.3	9.88	10.71	21.44
10.2	9.96	10.80	21.64
10.1	10.05	10.90	21.84
10.0	10.14	11.00	22.05
9.9	10.24	11.10	22.26
9.8	10.33	11.20	22.48
9.7	10.43	11.31	22.70
9.6	10.53	11.42	22.92
9.5	10.63	11.53	23.15
9.4	10.73	11.64	23.39
9.3	10.83	11.75	23.64
9.2	10.94	11.87	23.88
9.1	11.05	11.99	24.13
9.0	11.16	12.11	24.38
8.9	11.27	12.24	24.64
8.8	11.39	12.36	24.92
8.7	11.51	12.49	25.19
8.6	11.63	12.63	25.47
8.5	11.76	12.76	25.76
8.4	11.89	12.90	26.05
8.3	12.02	13.05	26.36
8.2	12.15	13.20	26.66
8.1	12.29	13.35	26.97
8.0	12.43	13.50	27.30
7.9	12.57	13.66	27.64
7.8	12.72	13.82	27.97
7.7	12.88	13.99	28.32

Note: For hand timing, add 0.15 to your time.

You cannot use your full speed factor at every distance. The farther you run, the less your speed helps you. In using the Energy Formula, you use a percentage of your Speed Factor according to the distance of your race. This table shows the ml/kg/min to use for each racing distance:

TO FIND YOUR SPEED FACTOR, KNOWING YOUR TOP SPEED

Your speed (meters/ sec)	800 75%	1500 60%	3000 40%	5000 30%	10,000 25%	Mara- thon 10%
10.6	15.3	12.2	)8.2	6.1	5.1	2.0
10.5	14.4	11.5	7.7	5.8	4.8	1.9
10.4	13.5	10.8	7.2	5.4	4.5	1.8
10.3	12.6	10.1	6.7	5.0	4.2	1.7
10.2	11.7	9.4	6.2	4.7	3.9	1.6
10.1	10.8	8.6	5.8	4.3	3.6	1.4
10.0	9.9	7.9	5.3	4.0	3.3	1.3
9.9	9.0	7.2	4.8	3.6	3.0	1.2
9.8	8.1	6.5	4.3	3.2	2.7	1.1
9.7	7.2	5.8	3.8	2.9	2.4	1.0
9.6	6.3	5.0	3.4	2.5	2.1	0.8
9.5	5.4	4.3	2.9	2.2	1.8	0.7
9.4	4.5	3.6	2.4	1.8	1.5	0.6
9.3	3.6	2.9	1.9	1.4	1.2	0.5
9.2	2.7	2.2	1.4	1.1	0.9	0.4
9.1	1.8	1.4	1.0	0.7	0.6	0.2
9.0	0.9	0.7	0.5	0.4	0.3	0.1
8.9	0	0	0	0	0	0
8.8	-0.9	-0.7	-0.5	-0.4	-0.3	-0.1
8.7	-1.8	-1.4	-1.0	-0.7	-0.6	-0.2
8.6	-2.7	-2.2	-1.4	-1.1	-0.9	-0.4
8.5	-3.6	-2.9	-1.9	-1.4	-1.2	-0.5
8.4	-4.5	-3.6	-2.4	-1.8	-1.5	-0.6
8.3	-5.4	-4.3	-2.9	-2.2	-1.8	-0.7
8.2	-6.3	-5.0	-3.4	-2.5	-2.1	-0.8
8.1	-7.2	-5.8	-3.8	-2.9	-2.4	-1.0
8.0	-8.1	-6.5	-4.3	-3.2	-2.7	-1.1
7.9	-9.0	-7.2	-4.8	-3.6	-3.0	-1.2

AC in the formula stands for Aerobic Capacity. This requires some explanation. First, you must understand what physiologists mean by "maximum oxygen uptake."

Physiologists in the laboratory can measure the amount of oxygen your body consumes. This is done by measuring the amount you inhale and exhale. They can measure this oxygen uptake while you are riding a stationary bicycle or running on a treadmill. This is a measurement of all the oxygen your cells can use.

Your total oxygen consumption is measured in liters per minute. (A liter is about one quart.) An average man consumes about one-fourth to one-third of a liter of oxygen while he is resting. His maximum consumption rises to as much as three liters per minute when he exercises as hard as he can. A really fit endurance athlete can use more than six liters of oxygen each minute.

A big man uses more oxygen than a small man, simply because he has more tissue demanding oxygen. Therefore, to make your oxygen uptake mean more, physiologists divide your oxygen consumption by your weight. Thus, a little man who can only consume five liters of oxygen per minute, can often outrun a big man who can consume six liters. This is because he can use more oxygen per pound of tissue.

Physiologists use kilograms instead of pounds. (A kilogram is 2.2046 pounds.) Your aerobic capacity is thus the milliliters of oxygen you can use in one minute for each kilogram of your body weight. (A milliliter (ml) is one-thousandth of a liter and approximately one cubic centimeter.) The little man (130 pounds, or 59 kilograms) who consumed five liters of oxygen in one minute had a maximum oxygen consumption of 84.7 ml/kg/min. The big man (190 pounds, or 86 kilograms) who used six liters had an oxygen consumption of only 69.8.

The little man's 84.7 is almost as high as any athlete has ever measured. If he had a minimum of running skill, he would be almost unbeatable in a marathon. If he had cycling skill, he would be a champion cyclist. If he had as much speed as Jim Ryun, he could run to a mile record.

The big man, with his maximum oxygen uptake of 69.8, would not be a good marathon runner, although he could run under three hours. If he had real speed, however, he could be a great half-miler.

Your maximum oxygen uptake is not the same as your aerobic capacity, although the two terms are sometimes carelessly reversed. Some of the oxygen you consume is not used in running:

• Your basal metabolism continues while you are running. This is normally subtracted from your maximum oxygen uptake.

• Your basal consumption of oxygen is nearly doubled during hard running.[80] Although this is part of your maximum oxygen uptake, it does not help you to run faster. This amounts to about 4 ml/kg/min.

• An unknown amount of oxygen is used, while you are running hard, to convert lactic acid to glycogen.[113]

Nobody can measure how much of your maximum oxygen uptake is used in those ways, but good runners show a constant rate of about 9 or 10 ml/kg/min.

Another factor enters the picture to make the physiologists' maximum oxygen uptake unreliable. Some reported figures are obviously wrong. In fact, some experiments have been done to show how various methods bring various results. Thus, Peter Snell's reported 72 ml/kg/min is obviously too low, and Don Lash's 81.5 is obviously too high.

One reason these maximum oxygen uptake figures are not always maximum is that some athletes do not punish themselves as hard as others in laboratory tests. The amount of lactic acid in the blood gives a good indication of how hard you try. When Kip Keino recorded his maximum oxygen uptake of 82.0, his lactic acid rose little more than two-thirds of the way toward the normal high.

Therefore, if you have what you consider to be a highly accurate maximum oxygen uptake, you can subtract 10 milliliters and obtain a close approximation of your aerobic capacity. By far the best way to obtain this figure is to solve for this unknown in the Energy Formula.

Laboratory tests show that you cannot produce your maximum oxygen uptake immediately. It takes several seconds to a minute, depending upon how hard you run. And, of course, if you are not using that oxygen, your aerobic energy is less than it will be when you are using your full oxygen capacity.

This lag in oxygen uptake poses a difficult problem in accounting for all the energy you use during a run. It would probably be impossible to solve except for the fact that you have some oxygen stored in your lungs, blood and cells when you begin to run. This oxygen is used by your muscles, but it is not measured as part of your oxygen uptake. As a result, you do not suffer an actual oxygen lag unless you start out at a fast pace.

In the Energy Formula, LA stands for lactic acid debt. Scientists have established the capacity of this chemical "energy bank" as 44 ml/kg. This 44 milliliters must be divided by the number of minutes in your race, since the Energy Formula uses milliliters per minute.

Several factors require us to change this maximum for each racing distance:

• If you never do any all-out running, you cannot have the full capacity of 44 ml/kg.

• In a race as short as 800 meters, you do not have time to use your full capacity. (Margaria established a maximum usage of 24 ml/kg/min.)

• There is evidence that your total lactic acid energy increases with the distance of your run because of gluconeogenesis, but little scientific evidence is available for use. Pending more exact information, this formula uses the total of 44 ml/kg through the mile distance. After four minutes of running, the formula adds 2 percent. (This checks with several scientific experiments as well as with empirical evidence from actual races.)

Therefore, these totals are assumed for various distances:

1500 — 44 ml/kg	10,000 — 65 ml/kg
Mile — 44	10 miles — 82
3000 — 47.5	20,000 — 92
5000 — 52.5	Marathon — 154

To use these totals in the Energy Formula, divide by the number of minutes in the race.

The symbol GD stands for glycogen deficit. This is how much you fall short of holding your aerobic capacity for the full distance of the race, beyond 3000 meters.

About half of your glycogen deficit can be explained with simple arithmetic as your loss of energy when your respiratory quotient gradually drops. As it moves from 1.0 down to as low as 0.7, the number of kilocalories of energy you receive from each liter of oxygen drops from about 5.05 to 4.60. The other half of the deficit may be explained by your curtailed efficiency from burning fat instead of carbohydrates. You are also handicapped by a build-up of metabolites, by added heat and by higher acidity in your blood.

Whatever the exact physiological explanation, or combination of reasons, no runner can avoid losing part of his aerobic capacity during each mile he runs beyond two. An exact figure is impossible, partly due to the difficulty most runners have in running their optimum times for longer distances, but from empirical evidence these figures work well for a general average of good runners:

For marathon specialists: GD = 0.3 ml per mile
For occasional marathoners: GD = 0.4 ml per mile
For 5000m-10,000m runners: GD = 0.5 ml per mile
For Mile-5000m runners: GD = 0.6 ml and up.

Al Salazar, at age 23, became the King of the Marathon by establishing the world-record time of 2:08:13. The native Cuban who was raised in Massachusetts, bettered Derek Clayton's mark of 2:08:33.6 at the 1981 New York City Marathon.

The Energy Formula is valuable to you in understanding how to train. Example of its various uses appear in chapters to follow.

Here are examples of how the formula fits, using experienced runners as subjects. Remember that few runners accomplish their optimum times at every distance. Another explanation of the formula's occasional failure to fit is the fact that a runner's condition varies from year to year and even from race to race.

JIM RYUN	800	1500	Mile	2-mile	5000
AC	68.0	68.0	68.0	68.0	68.0
LA	19.0	12.4	11.5	5.8	3.9
S (9.5)	5.4	4.3	4.3	2.9	2.2
GD	0	0	0	0	-0.8
Total	92.4	84.7	83.8	76.7	73.3
Equivalent	1:43.9	3:32.4	3:50.4	8:24.0	13:38.4
Actual	1:44.2e	3:33.1	3:51.1	8:25.1	13:47.8

KIP KEINO	1500	Mile	3000	5000	10,000
AC	71.5	71.5	71.5	71.5	71.5
LA	12.4	11.5	6.3	4.0	2.4
S (8.9)	0	0	0	0	0
GD	0	0	0	-0.6	-2.4
Total	83.9	83.0	77.8	74.9	71.5
Equivalent	3:34.8	3:52.8	7:42.6	13:21.0	27:58.2
Actual	3:34.9	3:53.1	7:39.6	13:24.2	28:06.4

RON CLARKE	2-mile	5000	10,000	10-mile	Marathon
AC	73.3	73.3	73.3	73.3	73.3
LA	5.9	4.0	2.4	1.7	1.2
S (8.5)	-1.9	-1.4	-1.2	-1.0	-0.5
GD	0	-0.5	-2.0	-4.0	-12.0
Total	77.3	75.4	72.5	70.0	62.0
Equivalent	8:19.8	13:15.6	27:35.4	46:00.0	2:16:06.6
Actual	8:19.6	13:16.6	27:39.4	47:12.8	2:20:26.8

FRANK

SHORTER	2-mile	5000	10,000	Marathon
AC	72.9	72.9	72.9	72.9
LA	5.9	4.0	2.4	1.2
S (8.4)	-2.4	-1.8	-1.5	-0.6
GD (0.35)	0	-0.3	-1.4	-8.4
Total	76.4	74.8	72.4	65.1
Equivalent	8:25.8	13:22.2	27:37.2	2:09:37.8
Actual	8:26.2	13:20e	27:46.0	2:10:30.0

ALBERTO

SALAZAR	Mile	3000	5000	10,000	Marathon
AC	74.0	74.0	74.0	74.0	74.0
LA	11.5	6.3	4.0	2.4	1.2
S (8.4)	-3.6	-2.4	-1.8	-1.5	-0.6
GD (0.35)	0	0	-0.3	-1.4	-8.4
Total	81.9	77.9	75.9	73.5	66.2
Equivalent	3:56	7:41	13:10.5	27:14	2:07:28
Actual		7:43.8	13:11.9	27:25.6	2:08:13

8

Combination Training

Your body can be trained to improve in many ways, all of them useful to you as a runner. In summary, here is a list of nine important capacities you must improve by training:

- Speed
- Strength
- Aerobic capacity
- Lactacid debt capacity
- Glycogen reserves
- Pace judgment
- Economy of effort
- Special skills
- Mental endurance

Each of these capacities can best be improved by concentrating on it alone. But while you are improving in one area, you are neglecting another. The art of training is to know *how much* of each kind of work you need, and *when*.

To know this, to make the right decisions about your training, you start by establishing goals. Your immediate goal depends upon your abilities, your state of training, your event and the season of the year.

You can decide that much easily. (You'll think more about it later, when you outline your program for the year.) There is, however, one other problem. Since you may have as many as all nine of the above capacities as goals, you have a problem of *combining*.

For example, you cannot ignore all running for three months while you build your strength through weight training. Nor can you succeed by doing your high lactacid training before any of the others.

You can gain on your opponents by combining your training methods in the best way. Combination training, like politics, is the art of the possible. Therefore, you must learn efficient methods of mixing your goals so as to reach all of them at the time of your most important race.

You can mix your goals in five different ways:

1) You can work toward one goal at one time of the year and change emphasis as the year progresses. For instance, you can use the Lydiard system and train aerobically for several months. Then you can change to strength training for a month or so, followed by speed training. Lydiard has been most successful, but if you want to compete year around you'll have to modify his program.

2) You can work toward one goal one day and another goal the next. This is particularly useful once you have reached racing fitness, but you may want to accomplish more than one thing at a time.

3) Two workouts a day can each aim for a different goal. Many successful runners do aerobic training in the morning and faster work in the afternoon. Even so, they must combine several goals into most afternoon workouts.

4) Divide your workout into parts, working first toward one goal and then toward another. This in one way of combining, but it is not the most efficient. The same principle applies: When you concentrate on one goal, you are neglecting the others.

5) Work toward multiple goals at the same time.

This last method of combined training resulted in the invention of interval training. To understand how to do the best job of combining you must be sure you understand interval training.

Everybody knows that to run intervals you run a certain distance, then walk or jog until it is time to run again, usually the same distance you ran. You repeat the run and the recovery a number of times, such as 10.

Everybody also knows you can vary the speed of your run, as well as its length. You can vary the activity of your recovery period, as well as its length. And you can vary the number of repetitions of your run.

Not everybody, however, knows how to fine-tune an interval workout so as to reach a specific goal or combination of goals. Let's analyze the five variables of interval training:

1) Pace. You have six speeds, which differ from the speeds of every other runner:

Sprint — as fast as you can run.

Fast Running — in between a sprint and your race pace.

Race Pace — your average pace for one of your events.

Borderline Running — up to your aerobic capacity.

Slow Running — definitely slower than borderline running.

Jog — too slow for proper form.

2) Length. You can jog, run slowly, or maintain a borderline pace indefinitely, for no lactic acid is produced. Only the three faster speeds are used in interval training, because the slower runs need not be broken into segments. You can maintain a sprint for a little longer than a half-minute. You can run your whole race at race pace. Your *fast* pace is about halfway between those two speeds.

You choose your length so that your chosen speed will build up the amount of lactic acid you want.

3) Type of recovery. During your recovery period you can do anything that will lower your lactacid level. If you are in shape to jog for hours, jogging provides the fastest recovery. Others do best with a slow walk, but you can stand, sit or lie down. Many runners jog merely to double the distance of their workouts.

4) Length of recovery. You vary your recovery period so as to control your level of lactic acid. There is no way of knowing exactly how fast your lactic acid level is reduced. From a combination of experimental and empirical evidence, here is a guess as to recovery time for experienced interval runners:

Length of recovery jog:	Lactacid Removed (Percent)
20 seconds	5
1 minute	12
2 minutes	21
3 minutes	29
4 minutes	36
5 minutes	43
10 minutes	67
15 minutes	81

Note: This means if you only accumulate up to 12 percent of your total lactacid capacity during your run, you can remove *all* of it in one minute. For an inkling of how quickly lactic acid can build up, Margaria[82] found 100 percent buildup in a little over 30 seconds of sprinting. Ten seconds at the same speed caused a buildup of less than 10 percent because of alactacid stores.

The most important part of your training plan is to decide upon how much lactacid buildup you want. Your recovery period should be designed to control it.

5) Number of repetitions. You repeat mainly to gain added mileage for aerobic purposes, or to practice the skills of speed running, or to build up lactic acid for anaerobic training. Thus, each added repetition merely intensifies whatever values you have decided to pursue in each segment of your workout.

If you know how to use these tools (speed, distance, recovery and repetitions) you can design a workout to meet almost any combination of goals.

You begin by listing all your goals and arranging them in order of priority. For example, if your first priority for this workout is speed, your second priority might be aerobic, anaerobic, strength or pace judgment. Each would result in a quite different workout.

In any workout where lactic acid is a factor — and this certainly includes most interval workouts — you cannot obtain exactly what you want by planning it in advance. Too many runners use another runner's workout. Too many coaches plan workouts that do not fit the runner. Too often, several teammates of varied abilities run the same workouts.

Ideally, *you* should decide the duration of your running segment and the length of your recovery, for only you can measure the extent of your lactacid buildup.

Runners adjust to rigid interval schedules by running their segments a second or two slower (or faster!) or by building up far more (or less) oxygen debt than desired. Thus, they miss their goals for the day.

To place control in the runner himself, fartlek was invented. From the Swedish words meaning, "speed play," fartlek is usually run in natural surroundings, but the same principles can be applied to training on the track.

Fartlek was meant to be the ideal workout, but a lazy runner can make it too easy and an overly ambitious runner can make it too difficult. Therefore, to get away from the distorted image of present-day fartlek, we should call it something like *controlled* running.

In controlled running, you run segments, as in interval training or fartlek. You choose your segments according to the priorities of your goals. And you recover according to how you feel, not to some pre-set pattern.

For example, if your first training goal is speed, your second goal is aerobic, and your third is anaerobic, you can accelerate up to sprint speed, hold it for a few yards, then slow to a jog. The length of your jog will depend upon your feelings. When you feel you have recovered enough to hold your lactic acid level at about 25 percent, you can run another segment.

When Filbert Bayi revolutionized the mile pace, Marty Liquori knew he needed more emphasis on speed: "I changed my workouts

Marty Liquori, with Jim Ryun and Tim Danielson, is one of only three American high school preps who has broken four minutes in the mile. Liquori's career extended from 1965 to 1980, and included the 1968 Olympic Games. Here he sets the American 5000-meter record.

from running, say, 15 quarters in 58 or 60. I changed it and did 20 220s in 27, because I found out that if I'm running against Bayi then the pace of the race is going to be 56, 57. . . It's impossible for me to do quarters at that pace in practice and do much more than five or six. So I cut down on the amount of distance I was covering and only did half of the distance, but did twice as many.''

You can learn to control your lactic acid level exactly as you learn to do it in a race. You know the tied-up feeling of an all-out 100 percent lactacid effort. You know the feeling of zero lactacid in running up to your borderline pace. It is up to you to estimate your feeling halfway between zero and 100 percent. Then you can divide those feelings again and know your feelings for approximately 25 percent and 75 percent.

Once you have learned controlled running, you can train for any combination of goals you wish.

PART TWO:

TRAINING FOR YOUR SPECIAL EVENT

9

Training According to Distance

You have been studying general principles of training. Now it is time to become more specific by examining your needs for your racing distance. When you understand your needs and compare them with your present ability, you will be able to plan your training program.

Every runner has a certain amount of both natural speed and natural endurance. To find your proper event you must strike a balance between these two.

It is easy to discover your natural speed. All you have to do is run a sprint race for time. If you are fast enough so that moderate training will put you under 10-flat for 100 yards, you have enough speed to be a top 800-meter runner. The slower you sprint, the farther you should race.

When you have chosen your distance, you must begin to set training goals and priorities. With priorities in mind, begin by analyzing each of the nine goals you must reach:

1) Aerobic Capacity. If you analyze the source of your racing energy for various distances, you'll see wide differences. Study the two figures below for each distance. One is the number of ml/kg/min necessary for a top performance. The other is an average figure for the aerobic capacity of a hypothetical champion at each distance.

Distance	Top Performance	AC of Champion
800	92.8	65
1500	84.8	68
5000	75.7	72
10,000	72.7	73
Marathon	65.5	73

The importance of your aerobic capacity is obvious. It is of extreme importance at 5000 meters or longer. Even at 800 meters, about 70 percent of your total energy is aerobic.

Here is another way to analyze it: How much has a good runner improved since his first year? How much of his improvement is credited to his aerobic capacity?

A study of the Energy Formula and empirical results shows us that good runners make most of their improvement in their aerobic capacity. About two-thirds of an 800-meter runner's improvement is from a stronger aerobic capacity, and it ranges up to 90 percent for longer distances. This study also shows a good runner improving aerobically by as much as 18 milliliters during his career. Reasonably then, any beginning runner can increase his aerobic capacity by 10 milliliters.

An increase of 10 milliliters means these improvements:

800 — 13 seconds
1500 — 30 seconds
5000 — 2 minutes
10,000 — 4½ minutes
Marathon — 25 minutes

The implications are obvious. You have more opportunity to exploit your aerobic capacity than any other capacity. This is where you can help yourself the most.

If you are a distance runner, your aerobic capacity is vital. If you are a miler, you cannot be good without developing it. Only an 800-meter runner with exceptional speed can succeed with an aerobic capacity as low as 60. (Among the few outstanding examples are Mal Whitfield, Tom Courtney and Alberto Juantorena.)

Conclusion: To succeed at any distance of 800 meters or longer, you should devote as much of your effort as possible toward increasing your aerobic capacity. Obviously, the longer your race the more effort you make.

2) Glycogen Capacity. The longer your race, the more glycogen you need. If you are an 800-meter runner or a miler, you need no special training to increase your glycogen deposits. The steeplechase distance of 3000 meters is about the distance where glycogen begins to become important. It makes a significant difference if you run 10,000 meters, and it is vital to marathoners.

Here are the approximate improvements you can make by increasing your glycogen capacity:

5000 — about 6 seconds

10,000 — about 45 seconds

Marathon — about 30 minutes

(Note: Those estimates are the difference between a fully developed glycogen capacity and that of a miler who does little long training.)

Therefore, the longer your race the more you should adopt these methods:

1. Long, steady runs to develop more glycogen deposits than interval running.

2. Single workouts to develop more glycogen than two-a-day or three-a-day workouts.

3. A long run (two or more hours) at a slow pace (slower than borderline) should be part of your schedule. These long runs should be at least weekly for marathoners and biweekly for 10,000-meter runners. Lydiard believes long runs even serve a purpose for the 800-meter runner during his aerobic period.

3) Anaerobic Capacity. Your opportunity for improvement of your anaerobic capacity is extremely limited.

This is not to say your lactacid capacity is unimportant. Without it, Juantorena could not run 800 meters in 2:10. In the marathon, Frank Shorter would be two or three minutes slower.

Even so, your lactacid *training effort* can make no more than about 2 percent improvement in your 800 time and almost none in your marathon time. This is because most of your lactacid capacity is already established during your aerobic training.

Beyond aerobic running, there are two methods of increasing your lactacid capacity:

1. Long runs, during which you build up a small, gradual oxygen debt, as in a marathon race. This is ample training for producing lactacid energy in a marathon, and it will probably develop most of the lactacid capacity you need for 5000 meters.

2. Short, hard runs, during which you may reach 100 percent of your lactacid capacity. Some of this type of training is necessary for success at 800 and 1500 meters. How much is a matter for debate.

Even if you believe much severe lactacid training is necessary for you to run 800 meters, you should reserve it for a short period before your racing season begins.

4) Strength. Another debate continues over how much strength training is best. Most authorities agree that you need more strength for shorter races.

You can increase the strength of your running muscles in three general ways:

1. Weight training during your off season.
2. Resistance running before your racing season.
3. A lighter dose of either or both throughout your year.

The latter course has several advantages. First, resistance running is more efficient if you have initially developed your muscles through scientific weight training. Second, an intense period of hill training can cause injuries, and it blocks you from other important training. Furthermore, if you have done weight training, you don't need as much resistance running.

Therefore, this program would seem advantageous:

1. Begin with intensive weight training until you double your strength.

2. Reduce it to about once a week, whatever is enough to maintain your doubled level of strength.

3. Introduce resistance running on hills early by running over small hills during aerobic training.

4. Gradually increase your hill running to the point where you run two or three fast but short bursts each day.

5. For cross-country runners, marathoners, and all others during the pre-speed period: Combine anaerobic training with hill strengthening for a few weeks before your speed sharpening period.

5) Speed. The simplest way to learn the value of speed is with arithmetic. Suppose runner A can sprint one meter per second faster than runner B. If all of that speed could be used in an 800, A would be 105 meters ahead of B in 105 seconds!

Nobody knows exactly how much of A's speed advantage is useful at 800 meters, but everybody knows it is a great advantage. The Energy Formula allows 75 percent, but it may vary for each individual.

Your speed becomes less useful as you race longer distances, until, in the marathon, it is estimated to be only 10 percent.

Therefore, an 800-meter runner places great emphasis on speedwork and a marathoner, little. And yet, distance runners know they can "sharpen" with a few weeks of speedwork and thus reduce their times on the order of 15 to 30 seconds for 10,000 meters.

Such a dramatic improvement, of course, is for runners who have been doing aerobic work with little or no speed training. If you include speed training earlier in your year, you will not need a crash program near the end.

Most of the speed used by an 800-meter runner is his natural speed, but you know you can increase whatever natural speed you have. Thus, the question becomes: How much can you improve your time with speed training?

The answer is impossible without knowing your condition at the start. For example, a 400-meter runner moving up to 800 in mid-season could gain nothing by more speedwork. A marathoner with no speedwork who wanted to prepare for a 10,000 could improve more than 20 seconds.

That example would require an improvement in top speed of about 0.3 meters per second. He would have to increase the distance he could sprint by about one foot per second, which is well within possible limits. It calls for an improvement in 100-meter time of about 0.45 seconds. Even a sprinter could expect to improve that much from the start of his training season.

Such an improvement in sprint time should improve your time at any distance:

800 — more than 3 seconds
1500 — about 5½ seconds
3000 — more than 9 seconds
5000 — about 11½ seconds
10,000 — about 22 seconds
Marathon — almost 40 seconds

Although it is obvious a shorter-distance runner has more to gain from speed training, it is also obvious that it is worthwhile to a 10,000-meter runner. Only a marathoner who never runs a shorter race can argue against speedwork.

6) Economy of Effort. Strive to make your running style more efficient. No one can argue against this fact: If you can run at the same speed while expending less energy, you can run farther at that speed. This, of course, results in faster times.

Since running efficiency cannot be measured, we can only guess at its value. You certainly cannot afford to waste energy in a marathon.

We can only guess at how much improvement might result from a more economical running style. Capozzoli's apparent improvement of 20 seconds in 5000 meters gives us a clue.

On the other hand, most runners learn to run with reasonable economy, and so they have much less potential improvement ahead of them. Your efforts at learning an economical stride will pay the greatest dividends at first. After you have become efficient, further training can only maintain your level.

7) Pace Judgment. It may seem as if pace judgment is like economy of effort — once learned is enough — but it is not true. Your pace-judgment needs are continually changing, and so you must relearn throughout your racing career.

You must relearn when you change events. You must relearn each time you improve significantly, because your increased ability calls for a faster pace. You must know different paces to fit different tactical situations, different tracks, different weather conditions and different goals.

Pace judgment is more important the longer your race, but an error can be fatal at 800 meters. And it is easier to maintain correct pace in longer races.

Therefore, no matter which distance you race, you must continually learn to judge pace and brush up on your knowledge before every important race.

8) Mental Endurance. Your ability to tolerate fatigue and the pain of all-out running depends upon many factors.

The first factor, obviously, is your physical condition. There is no need to condition your mental endurance while your physical condition is poor. On the contrary, many a young runner gives up the sport because he is asked to suffer too much before he is fit.

The process of training is the major portion of your mental toughening. Each training session adds to your mental endurance, unless it is too severe. Then, the trauma of overtraining may cause you to shy away from future hard work. You must harden yourself gradually. As your confidence increases, you will be able to handle more fatigue. Develop confidence gradually in training, then in racing, with easier efforts first.

In more important races, you will want to pay a higher price. Thus, an all-out effort to finish sixth in a dual meet may cause you to decide it is not worth the effort. But an all-out effort in the big race will probably bring you at least the satisfaction of a personal record.

In the dentist's chair, a tiny pain can seem large, but in a fight or a football game an equal pain goes unnoticed until the action ends. That is because your attention is elsewhere. In foot racing, the same pain in the excitement of the finishing drive seems small in comparison to the same effort in training.

The final drive on the last lap of any race, where you go deep into oxygen debt, is the most painful part of running, but you have excitement to carry you through. And you know it won't last long. You can tolerate a much greater pain if you know it will soon end.

The sustained fatigue of a distance race is much harder to tolerate. In an 800, you do not suffer until you are within about 300 meters of the end. In a marathon, you may hurt for the last six miles or more. This sustained fatigue requires the most mental control. You can practice ignoring it during long training runs, but you must be psychologically strong and highly motivated. In the final analysis, it is a question of mind over matter. The longer your race, the more it will pay you to learn the kind of mind control that enables a yogi to walk on hot coals.

If your race is a long one, gradually harden yourself by progressive additions. When you learn to tolerate one load of stress, increase it slightly.

9) Special Skills. You need to learn a few other skills for certain events. Such skills as starting, finishing, indoor racing, cross-country, and steeplechasing are discussed in the following pages.

The accompanying chart gives a percentage for each event. This percentage is the amount a beginning runner can improve in each capacity. The percentage does *not* show how much you can improve in each capacity. It begins with the amount a beginner must improve to reach top class. The figure on the chart shows what percentage of that total improvement can be made. For example, you can improve 200 percent or even 300 percent in the strength of one muscle, but the contribution of added strength to marathon improvement may be less than 2 percent.

Note: Only five of your capacities are listed on the chart. Three others (economy of effort, pace judgment and mental endurance) are not listed, for three reasons:

• Their effect on your final time cannot be measured. It is guessed that they contribute about 1 percent each.

• They have negative value. Your physiological condition gives you a certain potential. Failure to use these three capacities properly can only *detract* from your effort.

• They apply almost equally to all distances.

Also missing from this chart are Special Skills, for the first two reasons, above.

Grete Waitz was the first woman to break 2:30 in the marathon, doing it at the New York Marathon in 1980. In the late 1970s Waitz proved herself unbeatable at distances of more than 10 kilometers. She was also a five-time world cross-country champion.

CONTRIBUTION OF VARIOUS CAPACITIES
TO YOUR IMPROVEMENT

	800	1500	3000	5000	10,000	Marathon
Total improvement	0:25	1:10	2:40	5:30	13:00	1:23:00
Aerobic (percentages)	65	75	84	85	83	78
Glycogen	0	0	0	4	9	18
Anaerobic	11	6	3	2	1	0.4
Strength	5	5	4	3	3	1½
Speed	19	14	9	6	4	2

Note: The drop in percentage in aerobic capacity for the 10,000 and marathon is because glycogen is so important in those events. This conceals the fact that your aerobic capacity is most important in your longest races.

10

Skill Development

STARTING

The speed of your start can be of some importance in an 800. A sluggish start can cost you one-fifth of a second, which will look tremendously important at the break, or at the finish. And if your tactics call for you to take the lead, you must start fast.

Your starting position is a crouching lean, with one toe almost touching the starting line. Your other foot is extended to the rear. When the gun sounds, your first move is to bring your rear foot forward. Many runners jab backward with this foot and push off from it, losing time and efficiency. Your push comes from your front foot as your rear foot is swinging forward.

Perhaps the best way to learn the habit of bringing your rear foot forward with your first movement is to extend it far enough back so it can only move forward.

Starting is not difficult, but you should concentrate on it enough so that it comes naturally to you in a race. Every time you take a standing start, even when you are not planning to run fast, you should concentrate briefly on your start.

Do not make the mistake of putting all your energy into a hard drive to reach your racing speed. Some runners waste precious energy with inefficient form at the start. Try to move smoothly into your racing pace at the earliest possible moment without wasting excess energy. The worst fault is seen when a runner sprints out so fast that he must slow down to his racing pace. This will cost you dearly in the homestretch of an 800. Your start is of little importance in long races.

PACE JUDGMENT

Although pace judgment is more important in longer races, more mistakes are made in the 800. Apparently, many runners feel an excess of energy and that the race is so short they can start at any pace and still run well.

There is no way to learn to judge your pace other than to time your runs. If you will make your first run of every workout a timed effort from a regulation start, you can learn how to pace yourself at the start of your race. If many of your runs are timed during each workout, you can learn to pace yourself while in various stages of fatigue.

Make a game of it. Try to guess your time. When you guess wrong, discover why. Consider your state of training, your lactacid level, the wind, the temperature, condition of the running surface and humidity. These simple efforts will make you an expert at judging pace.

FINISHING

Probably 90 percent of all distance contests — man to man — are settled before the last lap, but almost no 800 races and few mile races are settled before the last curve.

Many runners, who are as good as their opponents in all other respects, lose because they have slower finishing kicks. In seeking improvement for your kick, consider the five factors that produce a good kick:

1) Endurance. In longer races, two runners are often close together until the last curve when one of them runs away from the other. Usually, that is because the winner has more endurance than the loser and could have run away from him much sooner if he had chosen to set a faster pace.

In middle-distance races, the same thing can happen, but the difference is not so marked, nor always so certain. If the pace is slow enough, a runner with greater speed sometimes wins over a runner with more endurance.

In a very slow race, such as 58/52 per lap for an 800, or 3:08/55 (last lap) for a mile, much more lactacid energy is saved for the finish. That is why you can run so much faster after a slow pace. As long as you have lactacid energy to supplement your aerobic capacity, you can run close to your full speed. Therefore, the higher your aerobic capacity, the more lactacid energy you can *save* before your kick. Most one-sided finishes are the result of one-sided endurance.

John Walker doesn't have to dwell on executing a proper finish in the 1976 Olympic Games 1500-meter race. The former mile world-record holder from New Zealand shows his relief winning the gold medal.

2) Tactics. In a hypothetical race at 800 meters, A leads at the first 200 in 24.5, while B is well back in 27.0. At the 400, A leads in 51.5, while B is still the same distance behind in 54.0. A runs the third 200 in 29.5, while B catches up with him by running another 27.0. Assuming they started with equal anaerobic energy, which runner has the most left?

The answer, of course, is B. That first 200 in 24.5 used much more lactacid energy than A could gain on B with his slow third 200. And there is no reason to believe the same principle does not work when A's first 200 is 25.5 instead of 24.5. Thus, B wins the race with what looks like a superior finishing kick.

Or, suppose you follow your opponent all the way, but you run wide on the turns, covering extra meters. All else being equal, the energy you wasted will make your kick look inferior. Many strong finishes in middle-distance races are the result of a wiser expenditure of energy.

3) Form. Theoretically, when you run faster you come closer to the form used by sprinters. You should run higher on your toes, lift your knees higher, stretch out for a longer stride, lean more, and swing your arms and hips more.

Milers usually do this, but half-milers who run their first 400 much faster than average pace usually do not. They actually lose more form and look more awkward as they slow down or fail to increase their speed.

This failure in their form is partly caused by their fatigue. They are close to tying up. But it is also partly because they run with a form close to their finishing form all the way; milers, at their slower pace, can make a greater change. A change in form means a change in some of the muscles being used, and new muscles may still have most of their glycogen supply. This may indicate that 800 runners would do well to use a shorter stride for the first lap or so before shifting gears for the final drive.

Your form for the final drive should not be a sprint stride, because that is inefficient. It wastes too much energy and you soon tie up. Your form should be close to the one you use for the first 200 of a 400 — a relaxed, "coasting" sprint.

You must relax all opposing muscles. Instead of a desperate, fighting struggle to force yourself faster, your finishing form should be a light, quick movement with almost all of your energy going into the fast movement of your legs.

Probably no man ever ran faster at top speed than Tommie Smith, and he looked loose and easy while pulling away from the other struggling sprinters. Another example was the beautifully light and swift form displayed by both Jim Ryun and Jim Grelle in the homestretch of the two-mile when they ran away from Kip Keino in 8:25.2. Peter Snell's form around the last curve also took on a grace and looked almost effortless as he ran away from his opponents.

In the finishing kick, your goal is to relax and hold your form rather than to bull your way forward with brute strength.

4) Psychological Attitude. You must admire the ability to come from behind in the homestretch. You need a "killer instinct" in which you take pride in your ability to defeat an opponent who stayed with you to the last stretch. And you need confidence in your kick.

You can develop confidence by outkicking other runners. You can start practicing in workout sprints against your teammates. Then stay behind inferior runners in unimportant races to build more confidence.

But remember that your purpose is to develop a good kick, not to fall into the habit of running from behind. Some middle-distance runners lose consistently because they decide almost every race with their finishing kick. Other runners have kicks, too. Your purpose is to develop enough kick so they cannot take advantage of your weakness.

5) Speed While Tired. Many runners have good kicks at the end of a tactical race where the pace was slower than average, but the champion can run fast while he is badly fatigued.

To run while fatigued, you must develop motor nerve responses that function when you are too tired to think. The last skill you learned is the first to fail when you are tired. Thus, an action you have practiced only rarely will fail when you need it most.

This means only one thing: You must practice form while you are exhausted. At every opportunity, when your lactic acid level approaches the maximum, you must think of your form. You should run "shadow races"[85] or actual races against other runners in training. These can be informal races where you go into the last curve in a bunch and then race for the tape.

Such finishing practice can be combined with your anaerobic training. In fact, it is probably the best way to make the discomfort of anaerobic training seem reasonably palatable.

If you are a long-distance runner who cannot afford to sacrifice mileage by running all-out very often, you can bring your speed to your maximum, make sure you are running with good form, and then slow down after about 30 yards. Even such a tiny bit of practice will help if you do it once a day.

George Germann explained his new finishing kick after he placed second in the 1965 AAU 880: "Last year I really got sick and tired of being passed in the stretch. I made up my mind to do something about it. In every workout since then, every time I ran 220 yards or longer, I always ran the final 110 yards extra hard. No matter how rugged the workout had been, or how tired I was, I honestly tried to run faster at the finish. It hurt quite a bit sometimes, but now it's all worth it."

It is quite possible that the most benefit middle-distance runners gain from their fast anaerobic training is this ability to sprint when tired.

INDOOR RACING

Although distance runners often run their fastest times indoors, competing on a short indoor track often presents problems for middle-distance runners. If you run with a long stride, you may never be as fast indoors as you are outdoors. To be successful indoors, you need a short, well-balanced stride, proper form on the turns, ability to accelerate rapidly and a special awareness of tactics.

• Short strides are valuable indoors because they are more efficient on the sharp turns. You can keep your balance easier. If you

An overview of the Cow Palace indoor track in San Francisco. The *Runner's World* indoor invitational in 1979 drew a stellar field that included Mary Decker, Grete Waitz and Steve Scott.

intend to learn both a short stride and a long stride, you should work on the short stride indoors. But if you want to use only a long stride, you can still improve your indoor racing by practicing proper form on the curves.

• Good turn running is mostly a matter of leaning and changing the direction of your feet. Start your lean one stride before you go into the curve and lean both forward and inward. Fix yourself into this position by keeping your eyes on the inside edge of the track about five yards ahead. Both of your feet should turn slightly to the left of normal.

If you do all your training indoors during the indoor season and run a full schedule of races indoors, you should have no problem. If your practice time on an indoor track is limited, you must make the most of it by doing your hard running on the curves.

• Acceleration is vital in indoor races, because the curves are too sharp for passing and the straightaways are short. Only with a quick increase of speed can you pass a runner under such a handicap. You can learn to accelerate by practicing it for a few steps in your anaerobic or speed training. The time to accelerate is when you come off the curve.

Indoor track meets allow the spectator to get close to the runners. Banked turns add to the excitement of watching an indoor meet. Because the track is small and narrow, action is often "bump-and-run." Craig Masback leads early-on in a middle-distance race.

• Tactics are the same as outdoors except for the sharp turns and short stretches. It is much better to be in the lead on an indoor track, because passing is much more difficult. From in front you can slow down on the curves and speed up on the straightaway to keep runners from passing. You must be much more alert indoors, both to hold the lead and to pass a runner. You must be ready to take advantage of your opponent if he slows the pace for a moment.

Fred Wilt has some tactical advice for indoor runners: "When racing at one mile or above on these tracks, the athlete should try to avoid following beyond two places behind the leader. The sharp, banked curves cause the leader to slow his speed slightly as he negotiates the curves, and unintentionally increase his speed as he comes out of the curve and enters the straightaway. The second runner will invariably slow his speed slightly more than the leader in negotiating the curve. The third runner a bit more, etc. The result is that if one is running fourth, fifth, or sixth position in single file, a mad dash is required after negotiating each curve to regain the same relative distance from the leader as prior to the curve. This might sound absurd or insignificant, but the athlete might try two miles with about 40 short rushes en route, and see how much kick he has left at the finish. This is called the 'whipcracker' effect." [139]

Practicing your indoor skills will sharpen your ability outdoors, for indoor racing exaggerates the importance of tactics, ability to accelerate, the short stride and keeping your wits about you.

STEEPLECHASE

You can be a steeplechaser if you can run a good two-mile and if you are agile, not too dependent on maintaining perfect form for your entire race, willing to do the extra work necessary to learn the skills and more courageous than most.

The 3000 need not be your best distance, but you should be geared somewhere between the mile and 10,000 meters. Your training, except for the skills you need to clear the hurdles and water jump, should be the same as for 3000 meters on the flat.

Agility is necessary to clear the jumps, although height is not. Many steeplechasers of international reputation have been between five feet five inches and five feet seven inches tall. The shorter you are, the more spring you need — relative to your height — because the hurdles are three feet high. You are allowed to vault over, using your hands, or put your foot on top and step over, but top competitors save time by hurdling.

A runner with excellent form gains many seconds by maintaining it and thus saving energy. But if you have difficulty regaining this form when you are thrown off stride, you will lose too much time, because the steeplechase contains 28 hurdles and seven water jumps. A successful cross-country runner, accustomed to changing stride, should be able to adapt more easily to the steeplechase.

If, in addition, you have the courage to hurdle and jump when you are dead tired, and if you have the ambition and desire to work at extra skills, then you have more chance than most runners to win honors. Because of these restrictions, most runners will not run the steeplechase, and so your chances of winning are relatively higher.

To learn the skills of steeplechasing, you must understand the theory, do the necessary special training, and practice. The theory of steeplechasing covers both hurdling and clearing the water jump.

To learn to hurdle, you should start like a beginning intermediate hurdler. You need not learn to maintain your step between hurdles, but you must learn to judge your distance from the hurdle and adjust your stride accordingly. It will help if you are adept with either foot leading. You need not learn to skim the hurdle closely, like a high hurdler, and yet you want some semblance of hurdle form. This includes a fairly straight lead leg and bringing the trail foot up close to your hip.

The water jump is more complicated. You must spring onto a barrier three feet high, then cross 12 feet of water. You do not have

Steeplechase is an event that requires leaping ability, endurance and raw courage. In the 3000-meter Olympic event, runners traverse a 12-foot-wide water barrier seven times. A view of the 1972 Olympic Trials in Eugene, Oregon.

to clear all of the water, like Amos Biwott, the 1968 Olympic champion. In fact, it cushions your landing if you land about two feet from the end of the water jump in a few inches of water.

The technique of the water jump involves keeping your center of gravity as near the same level as possible while going through the entire obstacle. Some pictures show steeplechasers have sprung up another two feet after leaving the three-foot barrier. That is much too high. You should avoid lifting your hips higher than they would be if you stood on top of the barrier. This can be done by going over the barrier in a crouch, keeping your supporting leg bent. Then, when you jump, you wait until your propulsion will move you horizontally, not vertically. This concentration on forward movement instead of upward movement saves strength and is faster.

A few more specific details of technique at the water jump:

• Your take-off should be about five feet from the barrier.

• You should not become dependent on a check mark during your run-up because as you become tired this will change.

• You should speed up and lengthen your stride before you take off, both to save speed loss and to gain more momentum.

• You should use your strongest leg on the barrier.

• The longer you keep your foot on the barrier, the more apt you are to jump forward instead of upward.

• After your lead foot hits the water, your trail leg must be brought forward almost as high as in hurdling so as to clear the water. You must come out running.

The importance of proper technique can be calculated. W.N. Coyne[27] puts the time-lag for each hurdle at 0.4 seconds and for each water jump at 1.1 seconds. This adds up to a total of 18.9 seconds. Another 16.1 seconds is added because of the fatigue of hurdling. Actually, good intermediate hurdlers can cut their time loss to less than 0.3 seconds per hurdle, and your time over the water jump can be reduced even more. A savings of one-tenth of a second per obstacle means three and one-half seconds for the entire race, plus whatever you save in fatigue.

You need some special strengthening exercises; bend and stretch like a hurdler and do bounding exercises like a triple jumper. Tony Saunders, British coach, says, "Weight training should consist of half-squats or step-ups, squat-jumps, power cleans, and alternate arm presses with dumbbells (control of the arms is a key factor in economical clearance.)"[118]

After you have done these exercises in the winter and have reached a reasonably good state of condition for running, you should practice the obstacles regularly. Probably the best way is to clear hurdles during your regular training, whether steady running or interval work. The more obstacles you clear in practice, the easier it will be in a race.

CROSS-COUNTRY

The purpose of cross-country running varies with different coaches and runners. If your main purpose in cross-country is to aid your track running the following spring, your emphasis will be on long aerobic training with only a little attention to racing. But if you are serious about your cross-country races, you will place more emphasis on the skills you need.

The serious cross-country competitor will practice his skills. The track runner who is not serious about cross-country competition can, however, gain from the varied terrain of cross-country. Muscles other than those used on the track are developed in a kind of resistance training, and they may be of value on the track, either as something to use when your regular muscle fibers are tired, or as a widening of the area free from fatigue.

An example of how different terrain uses different muscle action is the experience of Ron Clarke after setting a world record in 1965. He ran in the Australian cross-country championships at Perth. About half of the course was through deep sand, and he lost to a local unknown who practiced in the sand. Thus, you should practice over the kind of terrain you will cover in your races.

Cross-country is probably most visible on the collegiate level. Cold weather at the November 1979 NCAA championships forced runners to bundle up. Al Salazar, behind teammate Rudy Chapa (T-338), iced the victory.

The main difference between cross-country courses and tracks is hill running. When you run uphill you must lift your knees higher, but keep your stride shorter. Downhill, you should land heel first, with a longer stride, but you must keep your balance. Experimentation will teach you the best form.

The amount of time you practice on hills — as well as unusual terrain such as dirt roads, sand, plough, mud, woods and grass — depends upon how well you want to run on that surface. You must learn economy of effort under all conditions.

WARMUP AND WARMDOWN

No greater controversy rages around runners than over the question: How should I warm up?

Some strong arguments favor a thorough warmup:

• Fred Wilt lists 13 physiological adjustments that take place during a warmup. He advises about 15 minutes of activity.[141]

• Wing Commander P.R. Travers cites such changes and says, "A pilot experiment which I have been able to carry out suggests that these changes take at least 15 minutes to complete and have certainly occurred within 30 minutes."[132]

• Most runners warm up for extended periods, some for as long as an hour.

Others argue for less warmup:

• Dr. Peter Karpovich cites many experiments in which warmups were of no aid to runners. He wrote: "During the past 10 years, hundreds of tests have been performed in the author's laboratory, some with but most without warming up. No difference in endurance in treadmill running was observed."[64]

• Ed Winrow once defeated Amby Burfoot, Jerome Drayton, and Derek Clayton — three great marathoners — in a half-marathon. He said, "I was so relaxed I didn't even warm up for the race."

• John Landy: "In hot weather I think you can almost ignore the warmup in events of one mile and longer."[72]

Dr. Clayne Jensen, an objective investigator, wrote: "A number of studies indicate that warming up has no effect on performance and that it apparently does not influence the occurrence of injury . . . By studying the findings of the different research studies, it is apparent that the evidence favoring or disfavoring warmup does not clearly outweigh the evidence in the opposite direction . . . The recommendation of this author is to assume that warmup is beneficial, provided 1) it is specific to the particular performance, 2) it is timed so that its benefits are readily available at the beginning of the performance."[58]

Dr. Jensen means that you should warm up for running by running. And you should not sit around after your warmup while your body returns to its prewarmup state.

You can make some assumptions about warming up if you consider a few facts:

• The stiffness you feel before warmup varies according to your age, the temperature and the degree of difficulty of your last workout combined with the amount of rest since then. Thus, you not only vary from other individuals, but your own condition varies, and so you should use the warmup you feel you need in each situation.

• Some of the calisthenics you do as part of your warmup are done for purposes of flexibility and strengthening, not merely for warming up. These should not be considered part of your warmup, and some of them should not be used before a race. Common practice is to jog a mile or two and then do calisthenics, while the body loses the benefits it gained from jogging. It would seem more reasonable to do your calisthenics first. These would be the bending and stretching you need before running, plus any training exercises on non-race days.

• Your decision as to the running part of your warmup must include how far you run, how fast and how long before your race you stop running. Since there is no answer from science to these questions, you must use logic and common sense.

First, consider your supply of energy. If you are running a marathon, your supply of glycogen in your muscles is critical. Any running you do before the race depletes that supply. Therefore, before a marathon your warmup should be almost non-existent. Glycogen supply is also important in a 10,000-meter race, and so your warmup should not be extensive. In other words, the shorter your race, the more glycogen you can afford to spend on your warmup.

Your aerobic energy, on the contrary, is not limited in that way. In fact, if you run hard just before the start of the race you will have a greater oxygen uptake. This is supposed to be one of the chief purposes of your warmup. But consider the fact that your run just before racing has used up your immediately available supply of ATP and CP. Most physiologists do not seem to realize that most of the lag in your oxygen uptake is because your energy is coming instead from alactacid anaerobic sources. If those sources of energy were not available, your oxygen uptake would start sooner. This is proved by the fact that you reach your maximum oxygen uptake faster when you start out at a fast pace.

Thus, it is unimportant — within a reasonable range — how advanced your oxygen uptake is at the start of your race. But it is important that you have your maximum supply of anaerobic energy when you start. About two minutes of rest or little activity is enough to restore your alactacid energy, but removal of lactic acid is much slower.

Probably the most important consideration in your warmup is the presence of lactic acid. If you run some hard sprints during your warmup, as done by many runners, you build up lactic acid. Then you must rest for 15 minutes or more to get rid of most of it. Even then you will start the race with a small oxygen debt.

It is wasteful to start your race with any oxygen debt. For that reason, it seems unwise to do any hard sprinting in your warmup. (Note: A sprinter may sprint in his warmup because he does not need to conserve energy.)

As a distance runner, your fastest pace beneficial to you in your warmup may well be the pace at which you start your race. And this pace should be carried for only 50 yards or less in your warmup so that the energy for it can be supplied by your ATP and CP.

If you do not go into oxygen debt any further than that, you can repay almost all of it in three minutes. Therefore, it would seem logical to end your warmup about three minutes before your race with a very short run at your starting race pace. As for the total amount of running you do in your warmup, 15 minutes is ample, even for a two-mile race.

You can work out the details in a simple way. Assume at first that it is to your benefit to reduce the time of your warmup. Then, in your workouts, experiment with various warmups to find any differences in results. Keep in mind that many runners have run their best times with no warmup at all.

Your activity in the last three minutes between your warmup and your race may be important. If you are at complete rest you must surely lose some of the benefits of your warmup. If you move too fast, you will start your race without some of your potential anaerobic energy. Thus, a very light jog seems to be best.

In addition, there is some evidence that breathing to the point of slight hyperventilation can help you. Dr. Krustev wrote: "We know that a big percentage of the oxygen debt is formed at the very start of physical exertion, when the respiratory and blood systems gradually pick up intensity, until reaching peak point . . . Before the strenuous effort is made, several energetic inhalings and exhalings will assure an adequate preliminary saturation of the bloodstream with oxygen."[69]

Such hyperventilation will force oxygen into the "stagnant" far reaches of your alveoli and also remove carbon dioxide. Again, experimentation should be done, but you certainly cannot hurt yourself with half a dozen deep breaths, and it might help. Do not overdo hyperventilation to the point of dizziness.

After your race, you should warm down. Again, expert opinion varies. It is true that tests show you can remove lactic acid faster by jogging than by resting. And almost any runner can tell you that a warmdown speeds recovery and prevents stiffness. But Lydiard says you can do too much of it:

"I can't say I have quite the same views on warming down as it is practiced quite widely. The main essential after a race is to protect the overheated body against cold, and the best way to do that is to cover it up with warm clothing, rather than run around at a decreasing speed. Anyway, if you have run hard enough in the race, you won't be in the mood or condition to run around in a so-called warmdown . . . Aim to have a warm bath or shower as soon as possible after the race, and keep the body covered until you have it."[77]

Lasse Viren is the only runner to win both the 5000- and 10,000-meter events in two consecutive Olympic Games, 1972 and '76. He was a factor in the '80 Moscow Olympics 10,000, as well, but faded to fifth place. Viren was famous for peaking at the right time, and followed in the footsteps of another great Finnish runner, Paavo Nurmi.

PART THREE:

YOUR TRAINING PROGRAM

11

Endurance First

If you want to be a distance runner, endurance is your first consideration, for several reasons:

• It is most important. Your aerobic capacity, your glycogen reserves and your mental capacity to continue long running make up more than 90 percent of your ability as a two-miler, and well over 99 percent of your ability as a marathoner.

• This kind of endurance takes you longer to acquire than any of the other qualities you need. You can sharpen your speed or reach your anaerobic capacity in a few weeks. But your endurance continues to improve for years. Therefore, the sooner you start building your aerobic capacity, the faster you will be able to run *next* season.

• You need all the qualities of endurance — a strong heart, numerous capillaries, large glycogen reserves, psychological acceptance of the work, etc. — in order to make faster training possible. Speed training you could not handle at first becomes easy after you have a strong aerobic background. In fact, it is silly to start with a fast interval program before your body and mind are ready. That makes for short track careers.

Your present situation governs how you begin your training. If it is the middle of your racing season, it is too late to begin this program. If you are a veteran runner, you can decide for yourself on any changes, depending upon where you are in your season. You will benefit from any varied borderline running you can add.

Even an 800-meter runner needs aerobic training. Most of the best 800-meter runners have also been milers, with good aerobic capacities. Later on, you will consider an alternative to long runs, but there is no better way of building your aerobic capacity.

Ideally, your distance buildup should begin when your spring or summer racing season ends. Marty Liquori said, "You may run

134

your best race in June or July, but you start preparing for it the previous summer."[102]

The best preparation is probably varied borderline running, but you should work up to that gradually. If you are beginning your program soon after your regular season ended, your first period is Rest. This can be actual rest, from one day to a month. If you have injuries to heal, or if you need to recover from hard stress, or if you need a vacation to recoup mentally, you should take as many days off as you need. On the other hand, if you feel good and are eager to work toward next season, your Rest period can be jogging or slow running — the beginning of your Aerobic period.

The normal sequence of learning to run long distances is jogging, slow running, borderline running. Start where you are able. A beginner starts with jogging, but an eager veteran can go directly from competition to varied borderline running.

When you can jog comfortably for two hours, you can begin to increase your pace. Your goal now is to run slowly for two hours. Next, you increase your pace gradually until a pace of about seven minutes per mile is comfortable. Ideally, you should stick with this plan for as long as it takes.

During this increase, you should run farther, at a slower pace, on one day of each week. This is to increase your glycogen stores, which will, in turn, make the whole thing easier for you.

Your goal is to be able to run for two hours at a seven-minute mile pace almost daily with no strain or discomfort. This form of running is the only training done by some fairly successful long-distance runners. It has been popularized by Joe Henderson under the name of Long Slow Distance.[48] Amby Burfoot used it to win the Boston Marathon. Bob Deines and Ed Winrow gained notable success with it.

Henderson says long slow distance "isn't just a training method. It's a whole way of looking at the sport. Those who employ it are saying running is fun — all running, not just the competitive part that yields rewards. Training isn't an exhausting, anxiety-filled means to an end that's barely tolerated. The simple, unhurried, unworried, nearly painless daily tours of the countryside come to be as much fun in their own way as racing."[48]

The joys of long, slow running must be obvious to anyone aware of the thousands of road runners and the millions of joggers, and so emphasis should be placed on its value to distance runners, rather than its pleasure. If you enjoy it so much you never want to go on to harder training and greater glory, you will still be in excellent condition.

A word of warning to veteran runners: You can go out and run for two hours at a 7:00 pace without difficulty, but can you keep it up every day? There is a difference, as Ken Doherty explained: "Mastery over a given load of stress cannot be claimed the first time the load is carried, but only after it has been carried enough times and with enough freedom from strain to be met with full assurance and minimum stress. Psychological adaptation has now been added to physiological adaptation."[34]

It is important for you to develop your capillary system early, because you cannot do harder running until you can send the maximum amount of blood to all your working muscle fibers. It is inefficient, to say the least, to try to build a stronger heart before there is any place for your heart to pump your blood.

Tom Osler, another runner who advocates slow training, emphasizes that a slow pace avoids injury, promotes health, conditions your circulatory system, and conserves your adaptation energy.[97]

When you have mastered long, slow running (or sooner if something like cross-country season interferes and you make the decision to compromise), your next step is borderline running.

As explained in the section on endurance training, the pace of borderline running depends upon your condition. It is the pace that verges on the borderline of lactic acid production. This means your pace slows as your glycogen supply is depleted. Thus, at the start you run faster than your average marathon pace; at the end you are running slower. Your *average* borderline pace is slightly slower than your *average* marathon pace, because in a marathon you gain extra energy from lactic acid.

This pace is faster than your long, slow pace. In your two-hour long, slow runs your pulse rate may stay lower than 130 beats per minute. In borderline running, the average runner will have a pulse rate around 140 to 150. But you must not judge your pace by your pulse rate. You judge it by finding the fastest pace you can run and still feel as if you can run indefinitely. This "indefinite" feeling applies to your heart, breathing and general fatigue, but your legs will feel fatigue as they run out of glycogen. (This is an important reason for increasing your glycogen supply through long runs.)

Your next question about borderline running should be: How far shall I run? This question has no exact answer, for several reasons:

• You are a unique individual, physiologically and psychologically, and you'll have to experiment to find the answer.

• Your situation will determine how much time and energy you have available at this time of the year.

• Nobody knows exactly what is best.

The best answer, then, can only be: Run as many miles as you can without becoming too tired.

Since borderline running is a step up in your workload, you cannot expect to begin by running at that pace for two hours every day. Your goal in this phase of your training is to work toward that end. But since you are now training at a fixed pace, how can you put in the necessary miles?

The answer is to break up your day's work into two workouts. Your purpose in borderline running is to strengthen your heart, and so it seems likely that total time is more important than doing it all in one stretch. In other words, two hours of borderline running, broken into two runs, is worth much more than one hour in one run.

The longer your primary race, the farther you should run in each single run. Thus, a marathoner should work toward one long run per day as his routine workout, while a two-miler can take two shorter runs. This is because the two-miler is not so dependent upon building a large glycogen supply.

Toshihiko Seko, the great Japanese marathoner, is also fast at 10,000 meters. He takes two workouts almost every day of the year, 10-K to 15-K in the morning, and 20-K to 30-K in the afternoon, much of it close to a 5:00 pace.

This is the time you might want to establish the habit of the morning run. Every morning, before breakfast, you might run at your borderline pace, and faster. This habit will make certain your heart stays strong for the rest of your running career. No matter what your other workouts, you should retain this daily borderline run. (If you are a marathoner, of course, you merely extend this one run to a long distance, and it should not be *before* breakfast.)

During your borderline runs, you should concentrate on your running form until it feels as effortless as possible. If you concentrate too long, however, you will not like it. This intense concentration on your running should be for short periods so that eventually you will run at your best form with only occasional check ups necessary.

This is the time when you begin to practice the *art* of training. You know the principles of training and you know how much you'd like to run, but you have certain obstacles in your situation . . . especially in your fitness.

Probably the greatest art of training is in knowing how hard to train and how hard to rest. You will make mistakes in this, but little mistakes won't hurt you. If you train a little too hard one day, you can rest a little more the next. If you undertrain one day, you'll feel like doing more the next. But if you make a mistake continually, your running will suffer.

If you have to err on one side or the other, it is best, especially at the beginning of your career, to err on the side of undertraining. If you undertrain a little, the only possible harm is a delay in reaching your peak. But if you overtrain, you can end your career completely. Bill Bowerman, Oregon's highly successful coach, once said: "I heartily endorse Gosta Holmer's philosophy that the trainee should stop his workout feeling exhilarated and not exhausted."[15]

Until now, your running program has been simple. It has been a simple, easy progression from jogging to slow running to borderline running. But now the art of training enters the picture. You are going to have to make some adjustments:

• You must adjust to running many miles without undue fatigue.

• You must adjust to your racing schedule. If you started this program in June or July, you can go right into the fall cross-country season without major adjustments. But if you start racing, you must reduce your mileage. And you must practice other skills.

• You must add a few other types of training to your program, including pace running, some speedwork, strength running, and some anaerobic training.

• And since it is your final goal anyway, you must begin to change your borderline running into *varied* borderline running.

From now on you must do as much varied borderline running as you can. You should do something else only when necessary . . . for rest, for racing, for speed and anaerobic training. From now on, varied borderline running is the basic foundation of your training.

Varied borderline running is really a fartlek type of interval running, but with a minimum of swings from fast to slow. It eliminates sprinting and jogging, fast running and slow running. It has two speeds: borderline and pace. You run at your borderline speed most of the way. Whenever you feel like it, you put in a stretch of running at your race pace.

It sounds easy enough, but it requires more concentration than easier runs, and more endurance. It is not as comfortable as borderline running, because you build up a little lactic acid during your stretches of pace running. But with very little extra work it will prepare you to be as good a distance runner as your natural ability allows.

Varied borderline running is similar to the kind of training Gerry Lindgren preferred when he was becoming the fastest of all

American distance runners and second fastest three-miler of all-time. It is not far from the type of training world-record holder Ron Clarke used.

Nor is varied borderline running much different from the training used by the athletes with the greatest heart development — professional cyclists and cross-country skiers. Both put in several hours of long work each day, interspersed with some faster bursts. This is a fartlek type of training, with varying terrain and control of speed by the athlete, according to how he feels.

European editor of *Track & Field News,* Roberto Quercetani, reported[104] the training activities of the great professional cyclists of France, Italy and Belgium. After a month of rest when their racing season ends in mid-October, they put in about five months of preparatory training. For four months they ride three to four hours each day, in two sessions. Their pace is "about three-fourths effort" (well over 20 miles an hour as compared to "full speed" of 30 miles an hour). They mix in some "long sustained sprints and a little jogging." In the fifth month they add an hour to their training and increase their average speed and the amount of speedwork.

If you allow for the nature of bicycle races (which require sprints as well as 200-mile rides), the similarity between the cyclists' training and varied borderline running is obvious.

Ernst Van Aaken uses his "pure endurance method" to coach successful distance runners. He wrote: "Training after the 'pure endurance method' means daily endurance training at a certain steady state, in the most favorable respiratory conditions, without an increase of the initial oxygen debt and formation of lactic acid, and with an average pulse frequency of 130 per minute. This is achieved by long runs, at first with breaks (interval principle) and later on continuously, of between six and 50 miles [for the 800 meter up to the marathon distance]. At the end of the daily long runs there follows throughout the whole year a speed run over part of the racing distance, at a speed not exceeding the racing speed envisaged."[137]

Van Aaken's most famous pupil is Harald Norpoth, one of the fastest 3000- and 5000-meter runners of all time. Norpoth, in 1965, finished the last 600 meters of a 5000-meter race in 1:19.8! This is a 53.2 pace for a lap and a half, ample proof that endurance is far more important to your finishing kick than speed training.

Varied borderline running is similar to Van Aaken's method, except for the addition of more than one stretch of pace running per day. Each stretch of pace running can be as short as 50 yards, if you need to conserve energy.

Most of the good marathoners use some form of long running at a medium speed. Fred Wilt says of Derek Clayton, who ran 2:08:34, "He averages about 130 miles per week. He trains as he feels, but most of his runs are at a continuous, fast, nerve-splitting pace."[144] Clayton later raised his average to 160 miles per week.

Jerome Drayton, who ran marathons in 2:12:00 and 2:11:12.8 late in 1969, averaged 140 to 150 miles a week in twice-daily sessions. He usually started with a warmup pace of 7:00 per mile, but he speeded up. "I usually end up around 5:30 or even five minutes per mile all the time."[101]

Eamon O'Reilly, who set an American record with 2:11:12, trained for marathons with a seven- or eight-mile morning run and 10 to 15 miles in the afternoon. The Japanese run up to 18 miles a day in two sessions, with some of it at marathon pace.

Alberto Salazar runs several 17-milers at a 6:00 pace each week, and three times he runs about 15 miles with faster intervals throughout.

Dick Beardsley averaged 112 miles a week for seven until the week before he ran 2:08:53 at Boston.

Even Dave Moorcroft, a 3:49:34 miler and the 5000 world-record holder in 13:00.42, tries to average 90 to 100 miles each week, summer and winter. He does fast work on the track only twice weekly.

Arthur Lydiard advocates background training of 100 miles a week.[77] His men learn to run that distance in comfort and then begin to increase their pace without lengthening their distance. This mileage is done in only one run per day.

George Young's "new" training, which made him the second fastest two-miler of all time in 1968, included a seven- or eight-mile morning run at a speed close to borderline pace.

These examples of runners who owe much of their success to long, medium-speed running have been presented to give you confidence in this type of training. It is nothing new or revolutionary. Only the refined concept of varied borderline running is new. If you understand the principles of training, you should now have confidence that there is no better way to build the background of endurance you need to race successfully.

In the specific training programs later on, this endurance training will be called Aerobic. You aerobic training will change as you increase your capacity.

The Basic Aerobic Training Program

1. Jog until you can continue comfortably for two hours.
2. Run slowly until you can continue comfortably for two hours.

3. Mix borderline running into your slow running, with the eventual goal of being able to run at your borderline pace for two hours.

4. Increase the total number of miles per week you can run at your borderline pace until you reach your goal of 100 to 140 miles. You can run 100 miles a week in many ways. Simplest is a single run of 15 miles a day. It is easier if you break it into two runs, say six and nine miles, but you will not develop your capillaries and glycogen reserves as well. Or, using any combination, you can run farther than 15 miles one day and less the next. This probably serves you better than doing the same distance each day, because it touches more possible areas of improvement. Run longer when you feel like it; adjust your fatigue carryover by running shorter when you feel the need.

If you want to develop only your aerobic capacity, the program just mentioned is enough. But you also want to increase your glycogen capacity. Glycogen runs should be mixed into your Aerobic training:

Glycogen Training

1. After you have completed basic aerobic training, take time off from your borderline running about once every two weeks for a glycogen run.

2. Run at a slow pace until you are out of glycogen. You will recognize this point because your legs will feel "dead" even though your breathing is still easy. It is a terminal fatigue, somewhat like tying up during hard anaerobic running, but without the desperate gasping for air.

3. Repeat this long run, expecting to run a few minutes longer each time before you run out of glycogen.

4. A marathon runner should work up to six or seven hours before becoming satisfied. Seko of Japan said he ran a workout of nearly 50 miles at 7:15 pace, which took about six hours. An 800 runner can be satisfied with three hours.

5. This program should not be continued into your competitive season. Once you have increased your glycogen capacity to those limits, you can maintain it with long borderline runs. Once a year, perhaps, you will want to test yourself in a long, slow run.

Once you have reached your maximum mileage in borderline running (and glycogen reserves), you continue progressing even though your training program remains the same. This is because any improvement in your aerobic capacity increases the speed of your borderline pace. But there are other capacities to train. Therefore, you add these simultaneous efforts and call your program Aerobic.

Aerobic

1. Continue your basic borderline mileage, modified by these additions:

2. Introduce Varied Borderline running. Begin to run short segments of your borderline run at a faster pace. This faster pace is your race pace, and you hold it for only a reasonable distance. An 800 runner might hold his race pace for only 50 meters before resuming his borderline pace. A marathon runner might hold his race pace for as long as a mile at a stretch.

3. Continue your weight training.

4. Add hills to your runs in place of one or more segments of your varied borderline pace. The shorter your event, the steeper the hills. The longer your event, the longer the hills.

5. Practice your special skills as part of your running. These include steeplechase barriers, cross-country and indoor. This is *not* the period when you practice your finishing kick.

If you are an 800- to 1500-meter runner, you may choose to do controlled segments during part of your Aerobic period. By controlling your accumulation of lactic acid, you can run far enough to improve your aerobic capacity.

12

Strength Next

Your ultimate goal is to get the most from endurance and speed. After you have improved your aerobic capacity as much as possible in the time available, you must work toward speed.

Your next goal, after your Aerobic period, is Strength. This is the next logical step for two reasons: 1) Strength is necessary before you can reach top speed, and so it must precede speed. 2) Strength can be held indefinitely, whereas your speed and especially your lactacid capacity are of limited durability.

Of all the methods of strength training, perhaps the most dramatic is Lydiard's hill running. His runners begin this type of resistance running 16 weeks before their desired peak, and they do it for four weeks.

Their strength work consists of springing up a hill for half a mile with an exaggerated knee lift. Lydiard says, "The accent is on the springing action rather than on speed." This obviously develops muscle endurance as well as strength.

After doing this series of jumps up the hill, Peter Snell and the others jogged for a half-mile to recover. Then they ran down the hill fast, stretching their muscles loose once again. On the bottom they did speedwork for a total of about 440 yards. Thus, they combined speed and anaerobic training with strength work.

This series was run four times a day. In Finland, influenced by Lydiard, Pekka Vasala used a variation of this to become the 1972 Olympic champion at 1500 meters. During his Aerobic period, Vasala used hill springing once or twice a week, but with only 100 to 200 meters uphill. Then came a three-month period, through May, in which he sprang up longer hills three to five times a week. Emphasizing high knee lifts, Vasala continued using some hill springing until two weeks before the Olympics, where his final 800 meters was the fastest ever.

You should be careful to distinguish between Lydiard's hill springing and other hill training. Herb Elliott popularized sandhill running. In a primitive type of training characterized by all-out anaerobic training three days a week during his off season, Elliott did much of his hard running up an 80-foot sandhill where ordinary men could barely walk. Coach Percy Cerutty's instructions were: "Run up as hard as possible, walk down, and keep repeating until nearly dead." Elliott is said to have repeated this run 50 times in one workout.

Jim Ryun ran many 230-yard stretches up 25-degree Campanile Hill above the stadium at Kansas University. Emil Zatopek bounded through the snow. Gunder Hagg had his hilly 5000-meter fartlek course and often battled through snowdrifts to exhaustion. And thousands of runners labor over hills in cross-country running.

It is all resistance running, but, in some, the emphasis is on anaerobic training. In others, such as cross-country, there is not enough resistance for building full strength.

People who favor weight training say you can gain strength faster from weights without missing out on actual running. It is probably impossible to measure runners so as to know which way is best.

Lydiard said, "This schedule is a formidable and perhaps soul-destroying one and I am always careful to emphasize to athletes that it is also a shortcut to exceptional improvement on the track. It is certainly hard work, but the only other way to achieve the same effects would be to work just about as hard over a much longer period. The reward comes, of course, when the athlete goes on to the track to find that he can run quite fast times without a great effort, something he couldn't do over track-racing distances a mere six weeks earlier."[77]

On the other hand, there is something to be said for spreading your resistance running evenly over most of the year instead of confining it to one period. Strength is something you can work on at any time of the year. You can make an improvement in strength gradually over the whole year, or you can make the same improvement with four weeks of intensive work. But your motor nerves require more training. If you suspend most of your other running for four weeks while you do resistance running, you will need time to adjust your style to your new strength. On the contrary, if your strength training is fed in gradually over the entire year, your coordination keeps pace with it.

These are some of the advantages of Lydiard's hill springing: 1) You devote only four weeks of your year to it. 2) You develop capillaries in your running muscles, as well as strength. 3) You practice some speedwork at the same time, to aid your transition to speed. 4) You raise your anaerobic training level another step.

Here are some disadvantages: 1) During these four weeks your aerobic capacity probably slips a little. 2) Your running form at race pace is entirely neglected. 3) If you have several competitive seasons each year, you have difficulty fitting in this four-week period. 4) Some runners, such as John Walker, have injuries they blame on hill training.

Therefore, it seems reasonable to attempt to spread most of your strength training over your full training season, especially if you must race in more than one season per year.

1) Do weight training to the desired level of strength.

2) Retain that strength with weekly maintenance weight training.

3) Do some hill springing during your Aerobic period. One or two 50-meter hills each day will help.

4) The shorter your race, the more you should increase your hill springing, up to three or four 400-meter hills several times a week just before your Anaerobic period begins.

5) Estimate how much more you need and do Lydiard hill springing. You must obtain at least as much strength as Lydiard runners, whether you do it in eight months or four weeks.

Thus, on your training program, Strength is optional, depending upon how much you have obtained elsewhere and how much you need. In any case, it takes the place of your Aerobic period before you begin your Anaerobic period.

13

The Anaerobic and Speed Phase

You cannot plan your training program until you have decided how much anaerobic training is best for you.

From the chapter, "How To Train For Anaerobic Endurance," you learned that your lactacid capacity is limited, chemically. For that reason you do not need more than two months to reach your capacity.

You learned other reasons for limiting your hard anaerobic training: 1) The higher your lactacid level is allowed to rise, the less mileage you can run. 2) All-out running is extreme stress and can lead to failing adaptation. It lowers your hemoglobin count and your pH, and, therefore, your level of performance. 3) High lactacid training can hurt you psychologically. Countless thousands of runners have been driven away from the sport by the punishing demands of hard anaerobic training.

Dave Stephens of Australia, a world-record breaker at six miles whose training included almost no high lactacid running, wrote: "Pirie's training is all wrong. If I had done all he has done, and at those speeds, I'd be terribly disappointed with the results. I couldn't stand it, and neither could Zatopek, who has tried. I feel Pirie is punishing the oganism to the extreme. He is restricting the building-up process in his body. In other words, thrashing himself and getting nowhere."[130]

Dave Rankin, Purdue coach, wrote: "High school boys run too hard. I cannot say that the coaches work the boys too hard, but I do know that the work the boys have scheduled for themselves, from reading workouts of much older boys, have run their bodies down to the point of poor function. I sincerely feel this problem will continue to enlarge itself if the boys of high school age continue to try to pursue the interval or punishment system."[105]

Astrand and Rodahl wrote: "A training of the anaerobic motor power is important for many groups of athletes. Since this form of training is psychologically very exhausting, it should preferably not be introduced until a month or two prior to the competitive season."[4]

This is not to say you should avoid anaerobic training. You learned that your aerobic running trains the metabolic pathways necessary for anaerobic running. Varied borderline running adds some anaerobic training each time you run as fast as your race pace. Hill springing calls for a higher anaerobic level, and your Strength period boosts your lactacid capacity still more. Few runners go without racing of some kind during their entire training period, and these races raise their lactacid capacity still higher. You are probably at 95 percent of your lactacid capacity when you finish your Strength period. How do you gain the other 5 percent?

The art of training consists, in large part, of knowing how and when to include high lactacid running.

You do your hard, concentrated lactacid training after your Strength period and before your Racing period for these reasons: 1) You do not need it earlier. 2) You cannot hold your highest lactacid capacity for more than two or three months. 3) You need time after your Anaerobic period to rebuild your hemoglobin count and remove other stress symptoms before you can race at your best.

Your next decision is the length of your Anaerobic period. Keep in mind this principle: You do some anaerobic training year around. Your *Anaerobic period* is a time when you overtrain deliberately to make certain you raise your lactacid capacity to its maximum.

Of the slight amount of literature on the subject, Lydiard's statement rings truest: "I estimated that if we used anaerobic training for four weeks before a big race, this developed your anaerobic capacity to its maximum. The East Germans refined this and extended this period to five weeks, which is more correct because they test for blood pH levels. If an athlete does hard, anaerobic work one day, then they can analyze his blood the next and say, 'Well, you haven't recovered yet.' So they give him another day of easy training before hitting him with hard anaerobic work again. This stretched my four-week period out to five weeks. . . You need an exercise physiologist to control anaerobic training."[50]

There is another angle to your decision about the length of your Anaerobic period. If you are an 800-meter runner, your lactacid capacity is much more important to you than if you are a marathoner. The type of anaerobic reaction you need for a marathon is probably best developed by long runs at racing pace.

For the 800, you probably develop most by repeated oxygen debts.

Therefore, it seems logical that your Anaerobic period should be shorter as your event becomes longer. Perhaps only 800 and 1500 runners need the five-week period. For the 3000 and 5000, four weeks should be enough. Three weeks may be sufficient for the 10,000 and two weeks for the marathon.

Your next decision is how hard you should train each week. Your basic anaerobic workout is at the 8-level. This means you reach about 75 percent of your lactacid capacity several times during your workout. Obviously, you should not reach the 8-level every day. Every other day should be your maximum. Three times a week is enough for most good runners.

Each 8-level training day should be followed by a much easier day. You can choose these from 5-, 6-, or 7-levels. Your choice should depend upon how well you recover from your hard day. Begin with the 6-level (several segments controlled at the 50 percent level), and use the 5-level or aerobic training if you are too fatigued, or the 7-level if you feel too fresh. If a sports physiologist is available, have him take your hemoglobin count and your pH to tell you how well you recover.

Finally, you must decide upon which workouts you'll use during your Anaerobic period. Your primary goal is lactacid training, but you want to maintain your aerobic capacity and you need some speed to raise your lactic acid level. Therefore:

1) Continue your aerobic training each morning.

2) Combine anaerobic and speed training in the afternoon.

3) Reach the 8-level three times a week.

4) Use aerobic running or the 5-, 6-, or 7-level to "rest" between 8-level days.

Here are some of your choices for an 8-level anaerobic workout:

Sprint Segments. Sprint any distance and recover any distance, but try to control your maximum production of lactic acid to 75 percent.

Fast Segments. Use your "fast" speed (between race pace and a sprint). Run farther than in Sprint Segments, but hold to 75 percent LA.

Pace Segments. Again, any distance can be used (up to 80 percent of your race), as long as you control your lactic acid level.

Mixed Segments. You can vary your speeds and distances as long as your lactic acid is controlled.

Hill Springing. If you want more strength training, you can use hill springing, with your recovery cut short so as to hold a high lactacid level.

Finishing Practice. You can race the last part of your event against your teammates and repeat often enough to make it 8-level training.

On your last run of each 8-level day during your Anaerobic period, let your lactic acid rise toward the maximum.

For 6-level training, you can use the same workouts (except for Finishing Practice), if you hold your lactic acid to about 50 percent.

A 7-level workout gives you less opportunity for variety. You can reach 75 percent of your LA capacity with one time trial at about 80 percent of your racing distance, at race pace. Or, after any aerobic run or light interval workout, you can run at pace until your lactic acid level reaches 75 percent.

A 5-level workout is like a 7-level except for holding your lactic acid level to 50 percent. A trial at race pace should end at about 60 percent of your distance. (Note: These 5- and 7-level workouts do not apply to marathoners.)

Needless to say, you should vary your choice of 8-level workouts. You should not use the same one twice in one week. And since this is your first speedwork, you should probably not use Sprint Segments until the end of your second week.

A typical Anaerobic period program for one week could look like this:

Monday — A.M.: Aerobic.   P.M.: 8-level Anaerobic.

Tuesday — A.M.: Aerobic.   P.M.: 6-level Anaerobic.

Wednesday — A.M.: Aerobic.   P.M.: 8-level Anaerobic.

Thursday — A.M.: Aerobic.   P.M.: 6-level Anaerobic.

Friday — A.M.: Aerobic.   P.M.: 8-level Anaerobic.

Saturday — Long borderline run.

Sunday — A.M.: Aerobic.   P.M.: 6-level Anaerobic.

Choose your Controlled Segments for speed as well as variety. The distance of your segments will vary with the distance of your race. For example, in Pace Segments at the 8-level, an 800 runner might start with 640 meters at his race pace, then shorten it to avoid going over 75 percent LA. On the other hand, if a marathoner ran long segments of his race it would not be an interval workout. He should use his 5000 or 10,000 pace, with short recovery jogs. Thus, the 800 runner might cover about 5000 meters, not including his jogging, while the marathoner might run 15,000 to 20,000.

SPEED PERIOD

When you have developed your maximum endurance, your only means of further improvement is by increasing your speed. This seems obvious, and yet it raises the question, "Why do runners improve as the season goes along?" There are many answers to that question:

• Some runners do not improve.

• Many run their best race in the first third of their competitive season.

• Some improve because they were not fit when their season began.

• Some improve by increasing their speed.

• Some improve because they try harder in the important races.

• Some improve because they train through early races and only taper for the important races.

Thus, the only *real* improvement, other than from added endurance, comes from increased speed.

Once again, there is no exact method of measuring how much speedwork you need. From empirical evidence, it would appear that the equivalent of four weeks of fast running is enough before your competitive season.

You can measure your improvement in speed by timing yourself for 100, 200 or 400 meters. These sprint time trials can serve as part of your speed training as well as a test. When you cease to improve your sprint times, you can consider your Speed period as ended. Then you reduce your speedwork, but you continue to test. If your sprint times begin to slip, increase your speedwork again.

During your Anaerobic period you do considerable speedwork, simply because the two go together. Speed raises your lactic acid, and so it is good anaerobic training as well as speed training. Therefore, when you have completed your Anaerobic period you have probably completed most of your speedwork.

At the end of your Anaerobic period, you should be somewhat worn down from the stress of lactacid running. You probably need some "rest" before your competitive season begins. Therefore, a week of speed training with low lactacid levels seems wise.

Thus, your Speed period overlaps your Anaerobic period and extends one week beyond. Then, to be certain, you can do more speed training as part of your training during your racing season.

A variety of training can qualify as speedwork during your Speed week:

• Towing. This is the ideal time to try towing, before your season begins.

• Downhill sprinting. You have used fast, downhill running during your hill springing. Now do some downhill *sprinting.*

• Sprints. With enough rest between sprints, you can prevent your lactic acid from accumulating. These can be sprint trials or short sprint segments. Hold your lactic acid below 50 percent.

• Fast Segments. Controlled segments at the 4-level (25 percent).

• Pace Segments. Longer distance runners should use a shorter event for pace, since the emphasis is on speed this week. A marathoner might use his 5000 pace. During this particular week, use pace segments only as a "rest."

• Mixed Segments. Use any mixture of speeds, but control your runs and recoveries to hold your lactic acid at about 25 percent.

This Speed week is important, but it should be fun, a relief after your hard Anaerobic work. Mix your workouts, using a little of each every day. Limit your anaerobic running, but if you feel especially fresh at the end of the week you might run a 400 time trial.

14

Managing Your Competitive Season

You are now ready to race, but you are not quite ready to race at your best. You might be compared to a brand-new racing car that has been designed for great speeds and lasting qualities, but must be tested and adjusted to reach the fine tuning necessary before it can race at its best.

To reach your goals during your competitive season, you need the far-seeing executive ability of a corporate officer, hence the name of this chapter. *Managing* indicates that your most important job is to balance all your activities and make certain every one of them is accomplished properly.

Your major goal is to be at your best for your big race, but you have three minor goals that lead to your major goal:

1) Meet your objectives in all your other races.

2) Fine-tune your pace judgment and tactical ability.

3) Maintain all the capacities you have worked to attain (aerobic and glycogen, anaerobic, strength, speed and economy of effort, plus any special skills you need for your race).

Your first step is to outline your racing schedule, for this determines the amount of time and effort you can spend on training during this period. Designate each race as "unimportant," "medium," or "important." If your schedule progresses from unimportant races through medium and then to important, it is easier to manage than if they are mixed. This is because you need to rest for important races.

Rest is necessary before a race if you want to do your best. You need rest to restore the full oxygen-carrying capacity of your blood, your hormone supply, your glycogen stores and your mental desire to run. But sometimes your training is more important than your

152

race, because if you omit too much training now, you will not be as good later.

You must adjust to your races with the proper amount of rest. A rough rule of thumb might call for no rest before unimportant races, cut out about three-fourths of a day's work before a medium race, and a day and a half before an important race.

The better runner you are, the easier it is to manage this, because you can win most races without special effort. But if you are part of the silent majority who lose more than they win, you may want to make a full effort in one of the unimportant races. It may be your biggest success of the year.

Ideally, you will be better off if you do not have to run your hardest every week for the entire season. Few runners can do that and end with their best time of the year in the big race.

You can avoid the stress of all-out races by running some at a slow "tactical" pace or by eliminating your long finishing kick when you are an easy winner or a hopeless loser. You can also ease off on your stress by dropping down to a shorter race once or twice.

The number of times you avoid an all-out race depends upon your physical and psychological situation. Keep in mind that nobody can run his best for 10 weeks in a row.

You might plan your efforts in advance, including the amount of rest you intend to allow yourself before each race. This, of course, is subject to changes in your situation. If you run faster than you expected, you will want to make some changes. Injuries or illness will force changes. You may have to run harder than you expected, or you may develop an unexpected weakness that calls for a change in your plan.

The next step in your planning is to decide how much anaerobic training you will do, and on which days. The minimum amount of anaerobic work for 800 and 1500 runners during this period should be twice a week, with once a week for runners of longer distances.

One of these two should be your race. If you run all out in your race, it is a 9-level day. At distances over 3000 meters, you need a week to recover and so you need no severe anaerobic workouts. If you are an 800 or 1500 runner, you should have one hard race and one hard workout each week.

The day on which you do your hard anaerobic training is chosen as far away from your races as possible. If you race every Saturday, your anaerobic day should be Tuesday. If you must have two anaerobic days, Monday and Wednesday are probably best. Your problem is to avoid hard oxygen-debt days following each other.

You must also plan how to maintain your strength. You should probably do one day of weight training each week during this period. Some resistance running should also be done to maintain your special strength during the first part of your racing season. This might be some hill springing for 800 or 1500 runners, and uphill running for the longer events. You should give up all resistance running when your important races begin.

Another important goal is to learn pace judgment. Now that you are near your maximum endurance and speed, you can begin to develop a feel for your racing pace. All of your workouts at your race pace will help, *if* they are timed. You should also run the beginning of your race often in practice to check your time.

Another goal is to develop your finishing kick. Outside of races, your only opportunity to sprint while tired will come on your 8-level anaerobic day. You should finish with an all-out sprint.

When you have planned for everything else, you can consider the most important training you can do during this part of your year — speed and efficiency. Much of your running should be at race pace, but you need some faster runs to sharpen your speed.

In your speed workouts your goal is to increase your leg speed if possible and to increase your ability to use an efficient form while relaxing at high speed. Keep in mind that the ability to relax and conserve your energy is as important as having that energy available in the first place. A calorie saved is a calorie earned.

While doing all this fast running, you must avoid raising your lactic acid above moderate levels, except on your hard anaerobic day. Hold you LA level to 50 percent at the maximum. These controlled segments can be at any speed or varied speeds. Your progress should be from sprints, to fast runs, to race pace. This means you should do more sprinting at the first of your week and in the early part of your racing season. As you approach your highest possible leg speed, you will benefit more from practicing efficiency at your race pace.

You can think of an endless variety of ways to practice your speed. Perhaps it is best to include certain speedwork in each workout and use a variety of methods for the remainder of your training. You might like to have a fixed format that you can vary to fit your needs. Here is an example that is adaptable:

1) Start each workout with a formalized time trial for pace judgment. Warm up and start with a gun. Run about one-quarter of your race, with a maximum of 800 meters. Try to run exactly your desired pace for your race.

2) Rest at least three minutes. While fresh, run a sprint race for time or against opponents.

3) Rest at least five minutes. Do controlled segment running at fast speeds or race pace, and hold your lactacid level to about 50 percent on most days.

4) For your last run of the workout, do a group finishing race. Since this is your last run of the day you can allow your lactic acid to rise a little higher than 50 percent.

With this sort of mixture, you can meet all your needs for the competitive season. Limit your workouts to the 6-level except on Tuesday. Use any variety of speed workouts you wish in your controlled segments.

For the 5000 and 10,000, less speedwork is necessary. Tuesday, for example, could be a hard anaerobic distance run, including a steep climb. For the 10,000, one other afternoon can be a long run instead of segments. A pure marathoner may want to do only one afternoon of segment running each week or two.

If you emphasize sprinting in some workouts, that should be done early in the week. Increase your race pace practice as the race date nears.

An extremely important part of your racing season is staying healthy. You must watch for signs of stress, injury or illness, and be prepared to reduce your training enough to ward it off.

Soviet athletes are tested with urine and blood samples, plus EKGs and EEGs every other day. Former Soviet head coach Gavriil Korobkov said, "If you don't have this information, you can't coach."

You are much better off if you prevent poor health than if you have to cure it. Your best preventative measure is rest. Don't be afraid to use it, because at this point in your conditioning its benefits outweigh its drawbacks.

In managing your competitive season, you must constantly assess your condition and adjust your training accordingly. If you become too tired, cut back on your lactacid training. If you need more anaerobic endurance, add a little. If you are forced to race too hard one week, ease off a little the next. Look for anything you lack and work at it. Your goal is to be in the best possible condition one week prior to your important competition.

In addition to managing your training, you must compete. You should choose your priorities for each race from these:

- Win
- Run a fast time
- Train
- Practice pace and tactics
- Avoid injury or undue stress
- Fun

15

The Big Race

Your big race is one so important that you will do whatever you must to run well. In preparing for it, you will choose workouts that best prepare you for it, instead of being concerned with less important races before or after.

The most important thing you can do is rest.

To understand what rest does for you — in addition to previous physiological understanding — think for a moment about this artificial comparison: Imagine all your available energy as being in one container, like a gas tank. This is all you have to use in one race; the more energy you have to spend, the faster you can run a distance race.

You have trained for most of the year with the purpose of enlarging your gas tank. Each good session of varied borderline running has added to its capacity. Each long slow run has widened it. Each anaerobic run has deepened it. In each workout you used much of the energy in your tank so you could work hard enough to expand it a bit more. Now it is as large as you can make it for this season.

Your immediate concern is to make sure your tank is full. It does you no good to spend a year expanding your tank to a size 10 percent larger than last year if, when you need it most, your tank is only 85 percent full.

Your main concern at the time of your big race is to be sure your reservoir of energy is full.

Energy pours into your tank because your body is adapting to the stress of your training. Stress uses up some or all of the energy in your tank. Rest fills it. Therefore, the main concern before a big race is to get some quality rest.

156

The question is, how much rest is best? Nobody knows an answer that will apply to you in every situation. But the answer is undoubtedly more rest than most people believe.

If somebody took a poll of runners and coaches, a rest period of two days would probably be the favored answer. Some runners insist on full workouts until the day before a big race.

To convince yourself such a plan is foolish, consider these facts:

• Your blood's oxygen-carrying capacity is weakened by the stress of hard running. It takes several days of rest to bring it up to maximum.

• Your adrenal cortex is depleted by stress. It may take up to two weeks to replenish your supply of hormones after hard training.

• Your glycogen supply is depleted in a workout. It will increase for several days and then level off, if you rest.

• Your desire to run hard is diminished after a hard workout. Rest will revitalize your desire.

On the other hand, there are obvious limits to the time you should rest. Your problem, then, is to find the optimum duration for rest.

Since science has not yet answered that question, you should consider some empirical observations and some opinions before making your decision:

• Lydiard stated, "Over the last 10 days before the big race, it becomes essential to conserve energy and give the body a chance to recover from the hard work it has had."[77]

Lydiard's schedule for a 5000-meter runner advises these workouts for the six days before the race: 1) one-hour jog, 2) run 880 yards of 50-yard dashes, 3) one-hour jog, 4) three 220s at full effort, 5) one-hour jog, 6) half-hour jog. Keep in mind that a jog of one-half hour or an hour does little to deplete the energy of a distance runner in top condition. It is equal to complete rest for an untrained man.

• In Mihaly Igloi's system, "The final phase of training is race preparation. When maximum speed and endurance for the year have been reached, the volume and intensity are reduced to allow the muscles to regain their explosiveness and tone. Igloi usually gives six days of easy running before indoor and early outdoor races, and up to two weeks easy running before races in late season."[14]

• Before Roger Bannister ran the first mile under four minutes, in what was his fastest race, considering the weather conditions, he rested a full five days.

• Before Don Bowden became the first American to run under four minutes, and the only fast mile he ever ran, he rested four full days.

• Jim Ryun's light schedule for four days before his world-record 3:51.3 in 1966: 1) 4 x 150 yards, 4 x 120, 4 x 100, with like-distance jogs; 2) approximately his normal warmup; 3) same; 4) three miles easy.

• Gunder Hagg broke 10 world records in 82 days during 1942, but when possible he rested as many as four days in a row.

• Peter Snell merely "jogged around in the evenings" for four days before his world-record 3:54.1.

On the other hand, Herb Elliott set his world-record 3:54.5 with only one day's rest, and Kip Keino won the 1968 Olympic 1500 in his fastest-ever time after running three heats and two finals in the previous seven days.

These exceptions prove lack of proper rest before a race need not be fatal, but these runners may have run even faster if they had rested.

If you have six days after a medium-hard race, you might train once a day: 1) a slow run, slower than borderline pace, for about an hour. 2) several fast but short sprints to sharpen your speed. 3) several 200s at your race pace, but jog farther than usual between so as to avoid building up lactic acid. 4) a few race starts. (First 200 of your race, for pace and form, avoiding fatigue.) 5) warm up. 6) warm up.

You can do other workouts, of course, but that is about the general level of work you should maintain. Your goal is to rest enough to fill your tank with energy. Avoid high lactacid training.

PLANNING YOUR OWN TRAINING PROGRAM

You have been studying theories of training. Now it is time to put them all together into your own training program.

No two runners should train exactly alike; indeed, your own program should vary from year to year. Marty Liquori said, "My training in high school was very different from my training in college. And my training now doesn't resemble my training in college one bit."

Your program is easy to plan under ideal circumstances, but your own special situation and desires make it more complicated.

Start with the basic program that follows. Then make changes if you want to insert extra races or whole seasons of competitive racing. The following examples should help:

Your Basic Program

Rest: 1 week
Aerobic: As many weeks as possible
Anaerobic: Maximum of 5 weeks
                               (2 for marathon, etc.)
Speed: 1 week (after anaerobic)
Competitive season: (whatever you schedule)
Big race: (the most important week)

To Add Other Seasons

Important races should be preceded by anaerobic and speed
weeks. Unimportant races or seasons can involve easy workouts
with no extra anaerobic or speed training. You can prepare for other seasons according to their importance.

Here is an example of a complex season for a 1500-meter runner
who also wants to compete well in cross-country, indoors and in
Europe:

Week 1   Rest
Weeks 2-12   Aerobic ±
Weeks 13-14   Anaerobic and speed
Weeks 15-20   Cross-country season
Week 21   Big cross-country race
Weeks 22-27   Aerobic ±
Weeks 28-29   Anaerobic and speed
Weeks 30-34   Indoor season
Weeks 35-39   Aerobic ±
Weeks 40-41   Anaerobic and speed
Weeks 42-51   Competitive season
Week 52   Big race
Weeks 1-6   (of new year) European competition

Here is an example for a road runner who wants to compete all
year:
 • Do as much Aerobic ± training as possible.
 • Run hard once a week, in a race or workout.
 • Do speedwork once a week.
 • Add long glycogen-burning runs as your schedule permits.
Here is an example of competitive-season training for 800 meters:
Morning workout — Aerobic ± (varied borderline running or

controlled segments at race pace with lactic acid held to 25 percent).

Afternoon workouts might be mixed:

(1) Warm up and run first 200 of your race.

(2) Sprint 100 meters for time (200 on Tuesday).

(3) Controlled segments at the 6-level (8-level on Tuesday).

(4) One finishing kick.

On Sunday, eight to 10 miles at your borderline pace. Rest: none for unimportant races; Friday afternoon and Saturday morning for races of medium importance, and Friday morning, too, for important races.

With your knowledge and these examples, you are ready to create your own training program.

PART FOUR:

HOW TO RACE

16

Competitive Effort

Your success in a race depends upon four factors, in this descending order of importance:
- Your fitness as a result of your training.
- Your effort in this race, as a result of your desire and courage.
- Your ability to use your energy efficiently.
- Your tactics.

When you step up to the starting line for a race it is too late to do anything about your training. And if your condition at that moment is far different from that of your opponents, your other three qualities can make no significant difference. But whenever your condition is nearly the same as your opponent's, you can beat him by superior use of those other three factors.

Nobody knows exactly how important your mental processes are to your success in a distance race, but almost everybody knows they *are* important. Roger Bannister said: "Though physiology may indicate respiratory and circulatory limits to muscular effort, psychological and other factors beyond the ken of physiology set the razor's edge of defeat or victory and determine how closely an athlete approaches the absolute limits of performance."

Part of your ability to cope with the intricacies of mental control lies in your understanding, as Fred Wilt explains: "It might prove comforting to the younger athletes to realize that even the greatest athletes suffer extreme feelings of anxiety and helplessness prior to a race, and are often obsessed with an almost uncontrollable desire to withdraw from the race. Frequently even the best athletes will subconsciously seek socially acceptable reasons for withdrawing or quitting, and even go so far as to simulate illness or injury."[140]

Wilt points out that there is no known solution for this scared feeling. You must simply accept it.

Ken Doherty adds: "Excitement before an important race is necessary for best performance. It should be sufficient to arouse the emotions and release the emergency reservoirs of stored energy that have been established by training. It is worry and uncertainty that drain the energy, not eagerness and excitement. The runner who has lost the stimulus of excitement before a race is either stale or too far over the hill."[34]

"Of 10 runners or more that walk up to any starting line," Doherty claims, "all have the jitters — though of course in diferent ways and to different degrees. Amazingly, this is a fact that each of them overlooks; all tend to assume that he alone is nervous."[34]

Your proper emotion is excitement, not fear. Tension limits your release of energy and your running efficiency. Your attitude must be positive, not negative. You must be realistic about your ability and your chances in the race. Your hopes and emotions should extend only to the limits of your ability. Your attitude should be: "If I run this race to the best of my ability, I'll be pleased with the result." This should limit your fear.

Once you are in a race, your effort makes the most difference in your result. If you quit when you feel tired, you will not beat runners in your class. The difference between winning and losing is often the difference between comfort and discomfort.

Wilt lays it on the line: "You must use the mental factors involving courage, competitive instinct, subconscious desire for victory, capacity to suffer, ability to ignore pain, fearless determination, perserveance, tenacity, and just plain guts in order to transform training into racing success. There must be developed within yourself a certain callousness toward pain and fatigue — the ability or refusal to succumb to excruciating fatigue. You will find that the difference between the winner and the loser in middle- and long-distance racing is frequently the ability of the winner to ignore the same symptoms of fatigue that have caused others to yield. The winner has the same feelings of distress as the loser, but the winner fights through the pain barrier to victory."[140]

This may sound harsh to you, especially if you are a beginner and do not realize what strength you have in you. But after you have raced and trained for a while, you will begin to take pride in your courage. You will be most proud of those victories you win by out-fighting another runner.

Part of your fatigue will become a habit and you will ignore it with a certain contempt. But when you are racing your equals, much of your success will depend upon your fight against fatigue. The longer your race the more this is so.

Hyman and Tulloh commented: "There can be few experienced runners who have not been tired to the point of wanting to drop out. This is normal, but to give in to it can be disastrous . . . Once an athlete has given in to fatigue he has set a precedent which is easy to repeat . . . When in the closing stages it really hurts, it pays not to try to think about one's own troubles but to try to imagine those of one's fellow competitors."[56]

Ken Doherty amplified that thought: "The runner should think of others during the race — their position, their condition, their probable timing of tactics. It will keep his mind off his own fatigue and alert for quick decisions."[34]

Fatigue does not set in immediately, and so you need not worry, if you are a beginner, that you will suffer throughout the entire race. Ken Moore, one of the world's fastest marathoners and a fine writer, expressed his attitude well in *The Runner's World* of January 1970:

"To be effective over the last six miles, one must harbor some sort of emotional as well as physical reserve. An intensive, highly competitive frame of mind over the early part of the run seems to evaporate after 20 miles. So I prefer to begin in a low-key, sort of yawning-sleepy state of semiconsciousness. I watch the scenery and the other runners with appreciation rather than with any sort of competitive response. I chat with anyone so inclined. Later, entering the last six miles, I try to get enthusiastic about racing. A strong acceleration gives a lift and I can usually hold a new rhythm to the finish. It's more fun to pass people late in the race when it means something."

You must try to concentrate on something besides your fatigue . . . *anything* except your fatigue. An emotion, such as excitement, is the easiest way. Gerry Lindgren, Ron Clarke and many others were quite positive about the help they received from an enthusiastic crowd. Their emotions were aroused to such a point that they could ignore most fatigue. You can make use of this emotion yourelf with a little ingenuity.

A few people who are emotionally close to you may be of more help than the impersonal noise of a large crowd. If you have especially good emotional control you may be able to obtain this same result simply by *thinking* of those people and their reaction to your race.

You might imagine the rewards of your efforts. Think about your medal, about the story reporters will write, about your name and your time on best-performance lists. Think about what you have to gain, not what you have to lose. Positive thinking *does* have power.

One way to occupy your mind is to work on your lap times. A simple problem in arithmetic, such as 5:29.5 divided by five laps, will take only a few seconds if you are sitting in a chair doing nothing else. But while you are running, it might occupy your mind while you run one-quarter of a lap. If you try to anticipate your time and make a game of it, you'll forget even more fatigue.

Another way to keep your mind busy is to have mental checklists you can review in your mind. You should check your running form periodically. You can also check your tactical plan and your training program for the season, the year, and for your career. During long runs, you can think out non-running problems.

Even so, you are going to feel tired. That is the nature of this sport. You can delay your fatigue by running at an even pace. You can forget some of it by concentrating your mind elsewhere. You will gradually improve your tolerance of fatigue as you train. You will avoid extreme fatigue against poor runners or hopelessly superior runners. But at the end of a few important races you will need that non-physiological quality that accounts for so much of this world's glory . . . courage. And courage is up to you.

YOUR PLAN IS BASED ON PACE

Before you can make your plans for any race, you must understand pace. Your tactical plan should begin with selection of the best pace for this particular race.

The most efficient pace you can choose in order to run your best time is somewhere near even pace. Professor Reindell of Germany and his colleagues advocate an even pace. They claim any other pace is less efficient. Hyman and Tulloh concur: "Since the mechanical and physiological efficiency of an athlete is greatly impaired by fatigue, it follows that it is to the advantage of a distance runner to postpone fatigue for as long as possible. To achieve this, he must moderate his early pace." And, ". . . an even-paced runner who has relaxed early in the race will be able to use his conserved nervous energy to fight his tiring opponents in the closing stages."[56]

N.G. Ozolin of the Soviet Union: "The more steady the pace in a race, the easier it is to turn in one's best time, because changing the tempo interferes with the coordinating functions of the organs and systems. An even pace promotes an economical use of available energy, a better operation of the biochemical processes and, most important, it creates a more favorable situation for the central nervous system."[98]

The longer your race, the more important it is to stay near an even pace. American Buddy Edelen, formerly the fastest marathon runner in the world, made this point: "If one must err in pace judgment, far better he run the first half of his race too slow than too fast. It is difficult to know just what pace one can tolerate when running the marathon. Attempting a pace which is too ambitious usually results in disaster the last few miles."[37]

Vladimir Kuts, double Olympic champion in 1956, illustrated this point in his first attempt on Hagg's world record for 5000 meters. At 4000 meters he was seven seconds ahead of Hagg's pace, but he slowed so much he not only lost the record, he lost the race. "I rushed off from the start without estimating and budgeting my own energy properly."[71]

It is quite evident that if you run much of your race at a pace different from an even pace, you will not be able to run as fast for the entire race. But there is evidence that the most efficient pace is not exactly even. There are three parts of your race to consider — the start, the finish and the long middle — and each has its special problem.

Logically, you get the most out of yourself if you finish the race so tired you are unable to increase your pace, but this bit of logic is full of traps.

First, if you really have used all your energy, your pace will be slowing, not holding even. And when your glycogen supply is that far gone your running becomes much less efficient. Also, as your lactic acid increases, your will to run decreases. And there is a definite danger you will misjudge your pace and tie up.

Sid Robinson, who was elected to the U.S. Track and Field Hall of Fame for his studies of exercise physiology, explains: "In recent treadmill experiments on a good runner we have found that the energy cost of running is greatly increased by fatigue in the late stages of an exhausting run. . . It is obvious that the runner should pace himself so as to delay until near the end of the race the sudden increase in energy cost of running associated with great fatigue and high lactic acid concentration. If the first part of the race is run too fast, the runner may acquire most of his oxygen debt and be forced to run the remainder of the race with a high lactic acid, with his efficiency greatly reduced, and at a much slower pace."[107]

As you become more tired, your will to run decreases. In theory it may sound right, but when you attempt it you'll learn that the price is too high for anything except your one ultimate race. Peter Snell broke his own world record with a mile pace of 56.4, 57.7, 60.2,

59.8. His comments indicate the unpleasantness of such a pace:

". . . with 660 yards to go, the feared oxygen debt began to build up. Within the space of a second, my legs, which had been feeling so strong, began to cry out for relief. . . Even at this stage, I'd lost my relaxation. It was a straining effort to keep rhythm and pace. . . as I swung into the back straight, the last shreds of my concentration seemed to ebb away. . . the harder I fought the slower I seemed to be getting. . . the reserves had already been expended. There was nothing there. . . It was mechanical desperation running, completely without inspiration. . . almost ruinous mental and physical processes of that last lap. . . I had run the race wrong. . . I realized it more than anyone else. . . I also made up my mind there and then that I would never run another one like that."[128]

The long middle of your race consists of the whole distance minus less than a lap at the beginning and end. (This is only about 200 to 300 meters in an 800-meter race.) This is the part people are talking about when they advocate an even pace. And yet an even pace may not be best.

In races longer than 5000 meters, your diminishing glycogen supply is an important factor. When you start fresh you may be able to run at a 70-second pace without building up lactic acid. But after a few miles, when your glycogen supply has run down to the point where you are burning more fat than carbohydrate, you might build up lactic acid while running a 72-second pace. Although no physiological tests have been made to prove this point, it seems reasonable to assume that you are more efficient at a faster pace while you are burning carbohydrate and less efficient at a slower pace while burning fat. If so, a gradually decreasing speed over the bulk of the race may be the most efficient way to run. This may explain why even the best distance runners tend to decrease their pace. Rather than attributing any slowdown to fatigue, maybe we should see it as the most efficient way to run.

Even in a relatively short middle-distance race, your efficiency decreases as you produce lactic acid and metabolic wastes begin to plug up your energy pathways. You need more and more energy merely to maintain the same speed, and each increase in speed means less efficiency. Thus, the most efficient method would be to decrease your speed slightly during the middle part of your race.

As for the first half a lap or more of the race, there are conflicting opinions. Some physiologists have jumped to the conclusion that because your aerobic capacity does not function fully at first, you are wise to start slowly until it catches up. Some coaches advocate starting as near your even pace as possible to gain the most efficiency.

But some in-depth research by a track coack/physiologist seems to indicate otherwise. Jack Daniels[28] tested many of the best distance runners in the United States in 1968. He found that your oxygen consumption is slower to reach its peak with a slow start than with a faster start. At the same time, your oxygen deficit or lactic acid energy does not rise in exact proportion to your speed at the start. This is probably because your immediately available energy from ATP is used to supplement whatever energy is lacking. Thus, if you start slowly, your ATP supplements your lagging aerobic capacity. If you start faster, your ATP fills out instead of lactic acid.

This seems to mean that you are a little more efficient if you run your first half lap slightly faster than even pace. There is a physiological explanation of this seeming paradox. (ATP can be used at any rate of running speed, while neither your aerobic energy nor lactic acid energy can support your full speed.) Daniels' test proves this is so. And the empirical evidence from most races show that runners naturally start a little faster before settling into their steady pace.

Thus, the "natural" pace seems to have a sound basis for being called efficient, even though it strays from even pace. Your "natural" pace is one where you start somewhat faster than even pace. After half a lap you settle into a pace a little faster than average. You gradually decrease your pace to a little below average. Then, when you begin to race near the end, you increase your pace significantly.

Other paces to consider, in addition to even pace and natural pace, are the gradual increase, the gradual decrease, widely uneven pace, and "surging." The latter two are obviously inefficient, while the first two cannot possibly be as efficient as even pace or natural pace.

Your natural pace probably varies too much from even pace to be as efficient. For example, if even pace is 67 seconds per lap, a first lap of 61 and a last lap of 57 would be too different to be efficient. But if it is true that a tendency toward a natural pace is slightly better than an exactly even pace, then you should compromise a little. The question is, how far should you stray from even pace?

On the first lap, a time two seconds faster than your average pace does not seem like much. But this saving of time is done in the first 220 and you must make up another second for your standing start. Thus, two seconds is a significant difference on the first lap.

On your last lap, a time of seven or eight seconds faster than your average is probably too much faster to be efficient, and two seconds is too little. In the absence of any scientific evidence, a good guess might be four or five seconds faster than average for your most efficient last lap in distance runs.

Lap times do not tell the whole story in a mile race because a 58-second lap can be two 220s of 29 seconds each or one of 28 and one of 30. These world-record miles, however, show examples of natural pace:

Norman Tabor, 1915	58.0	67.0	68.0	59.6	4:12.6
Jules Ladoumegue, 1931	60.8	63.4	63.8	61.2	4:09.2
Jack Lovelock, 1933	61.4	62.2	65.1	58.9	4:07.6
Sydney Wooderson, 1937	58.6	64.0	64.6	59.4	4:06.4
Gunder Hagg, 1945	56.5	62.7	62.2	60.0	4:01.4
Roger Bannister, 1954	57.5	60.7	62.3	58.9	3:59.4
Derek Ibbotson, 1957	56.0	60.4	63.9	56.9	3:57.2
Herb Elliott, 1958	58.2	59.9	60.9	55.5	3:54.5
Michel Jazy, 1965	57.3	59.2	60.9	56.2	3:53.6[90]

Other mile records came close to the pattern. Ryun's 3:51.3, for example, missed only because of his slow start. The tendency is seen in almost all mile races; the "natural" pace comes naturally.

Ken Doherty supports: ". . . runners should conserve their anaerobic reserves until the later stages of the race. . . the long-held assumption that exactly maintained even pace is the most economical physiologically is incorrect."[34]

The important question: How far from even pace is the best natural pace? In a 4:00 mile, even pace would be four laps of 60 seconds each, or eight 220s of 30 seconds each. A first lap of 57 seconds seems too fast, as does a last lap of 56. This would result in an inefficient-sounding pace of 57-63-64-56.

Perhaps a slowing of half a second per 220 is enough. This is purely an arbitrary figure. A full second is too much and a fifth of a second is not enough. For a 4:00 mile, 220 times would be 29.0, 29.5, 30, 30.5, 31, 31.5, 29.5 and 29.0. Lap times would thus be 58.5, 60.5, 62.5 and 58.5. This seems reasonable, although highly unscientific.

Using the same system, here are 220 times adding up to a mile in 3:51.2, with Ryun's 3:51.3 splits underneath:

27.9	28.4	28.9	29.4	29.9	30.4	28.4	27.9
29.3	28.6	28.0	29.6	30.3	29.5	28.0	28.0

Note that except for Ryun's slow start and his hurried third 220 after he heard his lap time, he followed the natural pattern.

For the 880, using the same half-second change for each 220, the first 440 would be about one second faster than the second. As in the mile examples above, the usual 880 practice is to stray a little farther from even pace.

Of all the world records until Ryun's 1:44.9, only one other had a faster second half. Thomas Hampton's 1932 Olympic triumph in 1:49.8 was paced in 55.0 and 54.8. Ryun's record was paced in 53.3 and 51.6. Almost nobody has run as close to even pace as Wade Bell's remarkable splits in a 1:45.0 880 in 1967: 26.1, 26.3, 26.2, and 26.4.

From this empirical evidence it appears that the natural pace is close to ideal for the 800 and mile. In middle-distance races, a change of about half a second slower per 200 seems reasonable.

Note that the first 200 includes a standing start, and so your speed is actually much faster. To run at even pace, allowing for one second lost at the start, you would have to run 28, 27, 27, 27. Thus, the natural pace allows for a fast first 100 to 200, and if more speed is available at the finish, your last 200 can increase a little more.

Other methods of pacing your race, in addition to even pace and natural pace, are the gradual increase, the gradual decrease, and widely uneven pace. The latter is obviously the most inefficient, although Peter Snell used it when he set his world 880 record in 1962:

| 24.8 | 26.2 | 25.9 | 28.2 | 1:45.1 |

The gradual increase is seldom used in the 800, but a few milers have succeeded with it. Interestingly enough, it was Snell who set a world record with it while he was still relatively inexperienced, in 1962:

| 60.5 | 59.0 | 58.5 | 56.4 | 3:54.4 |

Kip Keino, who tried all kinds of paces, tried to break the world record with this pace and failed only near the end:

| 60.1 | 58.0 | 56.9 | 58.4 | 3:53.4 |

The gradual decrease comes naturally to many runners, for it is nothing more than the natural pace without an increase at the end. Many 800s are run this way, mainly because half-milers lack the aerobic power to run fast after their anaerobic power is used. Two examples of miles run in this manner are Andersson's world record — not technically correct because he was able to increase slightly at the finish — and a fast one by Keino:

Andersson,	1944	56.6	59.5	63.3	62.2	4:01.6
Keino,	1965	56.4	59.2	59.3	60.0	3:54.9

Natural pace in longer races shows a large change in pace, on the order of several seconds per mile. But it is obvious that the farther you run the less you can allow such a change. According to the Energy Formula, a 10,000-meter runner with highly developed glycogen stores would naturally run his sixth mile 20 seconds slower than his second mile. But such a change makes enough difference in running form so that efficiency may be lessened. Perhaps the 12-second change in Ron Clarke's world-record run is more ideal.

Vladimir Kuts favored a modified natural pace. He called it his "record tactic," but the dictates of competition forced him to speed up sooner in his great 13:35.0 of 1957. His second 1000 meters was his slowest and each succeeding 1000 became faster.

In planning your race pace, keep in mind that conditions vary. Do not be too rigid. Be flexible and consider the condition of the track, temperature, humidity, wind, and your opponents. If you are in a large field of runners, you will have less control over your pace than if there are only a few of you.

Your planned pace is only a guide, but you must start with pace in mind. It is where you begin your planning. If you understand natural pace, you will not be worried about small variations.

17

Conserving Energy

The whole purpose of planning a proper pace is to make the most efficient use of your energy. Think of your "energy tank" as containing a fixed amount of energy you can spend on your race. The most efficient way to spend your energy is to spread it almost evenly over your entire race. Whenever you spend more than this amount you are not receiving full value for your payment.

As an exaggerated example, to make this point obvious, imagine yourself running at an even pace of 70 seconds per lap. Suddenly you run a lap in 60. You gain about 60 yards on the field, but is it worth it?

You have depleted your glycogen supply drastically, and now you must burn more fat instead of glycogen. You not only need more oxygen, but your coordination suffers. Worst of all, you have used up a large portion of your remaining lactic acid supply. You must pay back far more than those 60 yards you gained in one lap.

Thus, the first principle of conservation is: Do not vary your pace more than necessary.

The second most important rule to remember: Run as close to the curb as possible. It is surprising how many world-class runners do not understand the reason for this. All it takes is some simple arithmetic. Basic to your understanding is one fact: For every inch you run wide on a turn, you must run *three* inches farther. In a 10,000-meter race, each inch costs you four yards in the whole race.

The track is measured 12 inches out from the curb. If you can run eight inches from the curb all the way, you can run 16 yards short of 10,000 meters. But the most important point is to avoid losing yards by running too wide.

Many runners like to run on an opponent's shoulder. To do this you must run about a foot and a half wide of your oponent. In a

10,000-meter race this would force you to run 72 yards farther than he does, merely to stay even with him.

A third rule to remember: Do not "race" your opponent until near the end in the 10,000. Somewhere in the last three laps you must start maneuvering for position. Until that time your primary objective is to conserve your energy. What good does it do you to pass two men and move up to the leader's shoulder with three miles left to run? All you do is waste extra energy.

One of the smartest runners from that standpoint was Bill Dellinger, three-time Olympian. Dellinger was content to hang back as much as five yards in the middle of most races. He had no tension from being too close to flying spikes. He lost no yardage by running wide. And he wasted no strength passing runners before the proper time.

This practice came in handy during the wild "surging" of the 1964 Olympic 5000 meters. Dellinger's superior tactics enabled him to beat Jazy, Keino and Clarke to the victory stand.

You should make a game of conservation. Try to expend less energy than your opponents while keeping close to them. If you stay back, poised and relaxed, you can enjoy watching their mistakes.

TACTICS

After you have decided upon your most energy-saving pace, the remainder of your tactics becomes the art of altering that pace in order to defeat your opponents.

To simplify your understanding of tactics, assume you are running against one opponent. For these hypothetical purposes, you should also assume you are of equal ability at this distance, because when one runner is much superior to another, any tactic will win.

There are at least five major tactics in distance races:

The Run-Away. If you are a 10,000-meter type in a 5000-meter race against a miler type who can equal you at 5000, you should use the Run-Away. You know your opponent has more speed and you have more aerobic capacity. The slower the pace, the more he can use his speed at the finish. Therefore, any pace slower than your ideal pace gives him an advantage.

If you run at your ideal pace or slightly faster, you force him beyond his aerobic capacity and he must use up his lactic-acid energy too soon. He will be unable to sprint at the end.

The Run-Away is commonly used in the 800, but the race is so short it does not reveal itself until near the end when the trailing runner fades away. One of the best examples in the 1500 was in the 1968 Olympics.

Kip Keino was running against Jim Ryun, who was not quite at his best because of illness, but still probably good enough to win at sea level. The favorite tactic for almost all runners at the high elevation of Mexico City in the 1968 Olympics was to run at a slow pace and settle it with a fast finish, but Keino knew better than to give Ryun that advantage.

Keino had no fear of the altitude because he had lived almost that high all his life. He said, "I knew Ryun had a very good kick so I prepared myself to have a big lead going into the final quarter." And that is exactly what he did. He followed a 56 first quarter and led at 800 meters in 1:55.3 and 1200 meters in 2:53.3. Ryun, about 20 yards behind at one point, never came closer than 12 yards to Keino.

No other tactic is used as often as the Run-Away in 10,000-meter races.

The Sitter. This is exactly the opposite situation from the Run-Away. If *you* are the faster type, you should keep the pace slow so as to use your kick, but it is difficult to slow an opponent who wants to go fast.

You can use two methods to slow the pace. 1) Take the lead and subtly slow the pace. 2) Allow your opponent to open a gap; he may decide he has enough lead and slow down a little.

In any case, even if he runs fast, you "sit" on him until it is time for your kick. This tactic is most often used by superior runners who want to win in the easiest possible way, but it has been used in some fast races: Jim Ryun completely smashed Kip Keino twice in 1967 with this tactic, including one world record. In 1934, Bill Bonthron, after trailing Glenn Cunningham by 40 yards in a world-record mile, came back and pressed Cunningham throughout to win the NCAA and AAU championships, the latter in world-record time.

The Surge. If you have done a lot of short interval work and your opponent has not, you can probably stand abrupt changes of pace better than he. If so, you can wear him out by surging in long races. Surging is seldom used in middle-distance races.

To surge, you increase the pace suddenly for about 100 meters. Then you slow your pace. How much you slow down depends upon your opponent. If he follows you closely, you should slow to a pace below even pace. But if an opponent continues at even pace, you should slow only to even pace, retaining your newly gained lead. Make him gain on you before you surge again, because if you do more surging than he does, he has the advantage.

The best-known examples of surging in big races took place in the 1956 Olympic 10,000 and the 1964 Olympic 5000. In 1956, Vladimir Kuts tried to shake off Gordon Pirie for 21 laps. Kuts broke into a near sprint several times and slowed almost to a jog a few times, but Pirie foolishly followed every move until he finally cracked and finished eighth. In 1964, Ron Clarke changed from faster than pace to slower than pace. He was his own chief victim and finished ninth, while Michel Jazy, who followed Clarke closely, faded to fourth.

The counter for the Surge is to continue running your own pace. In the 1956 Olympic 10,000, Jozsef Kovacs ran his own race, 10 seconds faster than he ever ran before, and finished only 45 yards behind Kuts, who ran 15 seconds slower than his previous best. In 1964, the successful runners were those who ran at nearer to even pace.

The Steal. If you are successful with the Steal, it will be because your opponent gives up. It is a bluff. At some point in the race you increase your speed above even pace and you get far enough ahead so that your opponent thinks he cannot beat you. If he slows down because of this attitude, you can finish ahead of him.

You can begin the Steal anywhere in the race, but the most common places are at the start and at a point between one-half and three-quarters of the full distance. Your opponent's counterattack against your Steal is to run his best pace. Your only chance, if you begin your Steal at the start, is if your opponent gives up hope.

The farther you run before you begin your bluff, the easier it is to fool your opponent. When he is tired and fighting to hold on, your confident increase of pace, especially if you do some expert acting, can discourage him completely. This maneuver is quite effective in the marathon.

A classic example of the Steal came in the 1960 Olympic 5000 meters. Murray Halberg feared the finishing kicks of Hans Grodotzki, Al Thomas and Sandor Iharos. With three laps to go, Halberg increased the pace sharply, from 66.9 to 61.1. His shocked rivals let him open a gap of 20 yards and they never caught him, even though he slowed to 66.3 and ran his last 200 meters in only 31.3.

The Long Drive. Sometimes you do not feel capable of either a faster pace than your opponent can stand or a better sprint finish. A tactic somewhat more sound than the Surge or the Steal is the Long Drive. In this, you start before you would begin a kick finish and you spread your remaining strength over the entire distance.

If you are capable of running your last three laps in 67, 67 and 59 for 3:13 in your normal finish, you can start your drive three laps from the finish and run 64, 64, 64 for 3:12. In addition to a faster time, you may make a successful Steal or Run Away. Since you open a gap before your opponent decides to follow, he must be superior to you to win.

Thus, the Long Drive combines some of the best features of the Steal, the Run Away and the Sitter. If you start your drive before your opponent is ready, you open an unexpected gap and deliver a psychological blow. It is like the Run Away tactic for a short distance. And, the Long Drive is a Sitter's kick finish extended to a longer distance.

You may well ask why use the Long Drive? Why not choose the best of the three types and use it? The answer brings us to the complicated part of tactical racing: In big races you are usually running against more than one opponent of ability similar to your own. Perhaps your best tactic against runner A is the Run Away, but your best chance against runner B is to be the Sitter. Instead of making the decision as to which one of them you want most to beat, you try the Long Drive in an effort to beat them both.

The best example of a long drive is the remarkable last 600 meters of Harald Norporth in 1:19.8 during a 5000-meter race. Norpoth would lose if he ran against Ron Clarke's Run-Away tactic, and he could be beaten by Michel Jazy in the sprint finish of a slow 5000. It is doubtful, however, that any man could match Norporth's last 600 meters. Thus, it is up to Norporh's opponents to force their own tactics upon him.

A good example shows how a long drive can make use of the principles of the Steal and the Run-Away. This is a description of the 1960 Olympic 1500:

"The Olympic 1500 meters is traditionally a tactical race, but Herb Elliott couldn't care less about tradition. The hook-nosed, stoop-shouldered 22-year-old in the green and yellow stripes of Australia knows only one tactic — to begin, in the third quarter of his race, a relentless, man-killing drive, powered by animal strength, thousands of miles of punishing training, and a brain insensitive to the subtleties of foot racing. Herb Elliott runs to win. . .

". . . around the curve he moved to fourth again and held it past the judges, moving up to third at 800 meters in 1:58.0. . .

"Then, quite unexpectedly, Elliott used his tactic. The pace had averaged 14.7 for each of the eight 100 meters, and the last two had been over 15 seconds. Suddenly, Elliott ran one in 13.2, and Olympic tradition vanished. . . what had been a bunched pack now became a long file of somewhat dismayed runners.

"Herb eased up a little, running the 200 meters around the curve and down the stretch in 28.8, but then the jangling of the bell signaled one lap to go and he picked up the pace, running the curve 100 meters in 14-flat. He had completed his third lap in 56 seconds, but this was Olympic competition and runners were still on his heels.

"Once again he picked up the killing pace, storming down the backstretch in 13.6. . . Elliott now had an eight-yard lead, but he sped around the curve 100 in another 13.6, increasing his lead to about 15 yards in the stretch. Then his pace slowed. He appeared to be trying, but he had given too much. He was straining at the tape and his last 100 had slowed slightly to 14.4. He broke his own world record of 3:36 by four-tenths, winning by about 20 yards, the largest winning margin in Olympic 1500 history. His last 400 meters was in 55.6, his last 800 in 1:52.8."[91]

In spite of easing up somewhat after that 13.2 100 meters, which began his drive, Elliott's long drive lasted 700 meters. He could have waited for 100 meters and avoided tying up at the finish, but that is always a guess. Sometimes it is better to overestimate your ability; it can be a real shock to your opponents.

In a big race you cannot have it all your way. Your basic tactic, then, should be to run your own best race. A win-or-nothing tactic may be wise against a single opponent, but in the Olympics it would be foolish. In the Olympics, or any big race, you should run your best time and try for the highest possible place. Even so, certain small tactics can be of value toward the end of any race where several runners together are of nearly equal ability. Here are five to remember:

Avoid a Box. During the first half of any race and up to the last lap of most races, it cannot hurt you to be boxed in as long as all of you are running at the same pace. Your problem until the last lap is to conserve your energy. But on the last lap, you must avoid a box.

The best way to avoid a box is to be in the lead. If, for any reason, you are not in the lead, the next best way is to run on your opponent's shoulder. This means you have room to pass him if another runner comes alongside you. You are foolish to run extra distance around a curve early in a race, but sometimes on the last lap you are foolish not to.

When you approach the final curve of a race, you should estimate your situation. If one man is ahead of you and he is the best man in the race, you are safe unless he unexpectedly has a bad day. If he is not necessarily the best in the race, but the others are strung out in single file behind, you are reasonably safe as long as you stay alert. This is because when another runner moves up on your right you can edge out gradually, so as not to foul him, and take a position on the leader's shoulder.

But if the field is bunched, you are in danger. In the first place you should not allow a pace that will bring the field to the last turn in a bunch, unless you are in the lead. If they are better than you and you cannot help it, don't worry about a box. But if you are all close to equal and being boxed can change your position two or three places, you must stay out of it. Even if you have to run wide around the last curve, you should do it as long as you can gain.

Sometimes you are hopelessly behind going into the last curve and the runners in front stack up on you three wide. If you are still full of energy and only need room to run, get into position behind the best of the three runners and follow him when he kicks.

When you consider all the bad situations you might find yourself in while being boxed, you can understand why most 800 races are run at a gradually decreasing pace. With a strong field it is sometimes a tactical fight all the way.

Lead Into the Last Turn. If you are in the lead going into the last turn, you have a big advantage. To pass you on the curve, your opponent must spend much extra energy. For example, if he uses 50 meters to come from a meter and a half behind you to a meter and a half ahead, he must run 6 percent faster. But on the curve he must run at least 10 percent faster because of the extra ground he must cover. If he is much better than you are at this particular time, he will win anyway. If not, he cannot afford to waste that much energy.

If he waits until the home stretch, he will have 50 to 80 meters in which to gain a little more than a meter and à half on you. This means he must put out 2 percent to 3 percent more than you. That does not seem like much, but keep in mind that the difference between a lap in 70 seconds and one in 68.6 is only 2 percent.

You should also consider the alternative. If you trail him into the homestretch, *you* must make up that meter and a half. Therefore, the real difference between the two positions is three meters. Thus, if you trail into the homestretch, you must be three meters better than if you lead.

This fact is perfectly obvious to anyone who has run indoors. You cannot come from behind in the homestretch of an indoor race, with its short straightaway, unless you are far superior. On a longer homestretch, this fact is not so obvious. In all-out sprints, this 4 to 6 percent difference is most often the difference between winning and losing.

A study of some 100 important mile and 1500 races over a period of about 10 years proves empirically the value of leading near the end. The runner who led into the homestretch won 82 percent of those races! And the runner who led into the last curve won 72 percent.

Pass Big. You can decide to lead into the last turn, but your opponent has something to say about it. He may not want you to lead. Therefore, when you pass him, don't try to edge past with a minimum of effort. With 300 yards to go, you may have only 50 yards of sprint left in you, but it is worth using 10 or 15 yards of it to be sure you get past him. And sometimes such a burst has a psychological effect on your opponent, and you can steal the race. If you do not pass big, your opponent will have time to increase his pace and hold you off.

Your temptation will be to sneak up to his shoulder before you put on your burst, but if you get too close he will see you, or hear you, or hear the crowd's roar, and he will be alerted. Instead, you should start from at least a meter and a half back, where you normally run. Then, by the time he knows you are coming, you will be going too fast for him to react.

The most efficient way to take the lead is to pass during a lull. Somewhere during almost every race the pace slows considerably because the runners are tired and it is not yet time to start the final drive. This lull may last for 100 meters and the time for that 100 may be a half-second to a full second slower than the average pace for the race. The faster the early pace, the more certain you can be that a lull will take place. And a fast early pace means the lull will be at a much slower pace.

In important races, with great runners in the field, a lull seldom takes place in the last quarter of the race. The most likely places are the next to last curve in an 800, somewhere on the third lap of a mile, and with three to five laps to go in longer races. After you have had some experience, and if you are alert for it, you can sense the lull. That is the best time for you to pass.

If the pace slows by as much as a half-second in 100 meters, which is quite common, you can gain three or four meters with no increase in pace. If the pace slows a full second, you need only a slight increase in pace to gain 10 meters on the field.

Instead of slowing and resting with the others, you should take advantage of this lull and pass the slowing runners. This will give you a great advantage in middle-distance races.

The lull during the 1964 Olympic 800 came on the next to last turn. Peter Snell was badly boxed in sixth place and he needed the entire turn to work himself into position for his big move. Bill Crothers, in fourth place, could have moved during that lull. He could have led into the last curve and Snell could then either run wide or trail Crothers into the homestretch. Since Crothers was good enough to gain on Snell in the stretch, Snell may have had difficulty winning if Crothers had moved during the lull.

Run Him Wide. If you are leading and your opponent tries to take the lead into the last turn, increase your pace just enough to keep him at your side. Then he must either drop back or run three yards farther around the curve. That three-yard advantage will come in handy down the homestretch.

Your main problem is that he may pass big. On the last lap — particularly on the last backstretch — you must be alert for this tactic by your opponent. Sometimes the shadows allow you to watch his position. Sometimes the crowd is quiet enough so that you can hear him. But usually you will not know he is coming until you see him.

Thus, it is important to watch for him. If your peripheral vision is normal, you can catch sight of his feet while he is still about two feet behind you. By turning your head slightly, you can see him a full meter sooner. If you lower your head, you can see him even sooner. Perhaps the best way to peek is to lower your head and turn it slightly to your right during the crucial seconds on the backstretch.

Surprise From Behind. Sometimes both you and your opponent are so tired and so evenly matched that each of you has only one small sprint left. In that case, the man behind has a certain psychological advantage. You have a target to hang onto in your fatigue. You can see him and he is your target. But he cannot see you and if you do not move alongside he does not feel so threatened. He is so tired he is willing to run as easily as possible to win.

It is not a commonly discussed fact, but almost no runner uses every last ounce of his energy unless there is another runner near him. The pain of a 100 percent effort is too much to give unless it is absolutely necessary. This fact can be documented:

Peter Snell often stated that he had a reserve he would never use unless pressed by an opponent in the homestretch. Michel Jazy indicated this after his surprise second in the 1960 Olympic 1500. Twenty yards behind Elliott in the stretch and a safe six ahead of Istvan Rozsavolgyi, Jazy missed the European record by three-tenths of a second. He said, "I suffered the woes of Hell down the homestretch, yet I think I would have tortured myself to go a bit faster if I had known I was that close to the European record."

The most vivid illustration of the fact that the front man does not put out all he has until threatened came during the big races of the 1963 season in California. At the Coliseum Relays, Dyrol Burleson waited until Snell kicked first and then he came back and lost by only four feet. At the Compton Invitational, in a fast race, Snell pulled away from Burleson in the stretch and Burleson knew he was beaten. He slowed visibly and he was nipped by Jim Beatty for second. Beatty collected a new American record of 3:55.5 solely because he had a target and Burleson did not.

Thus, it is sometimes to your advantage not to threaten your front-running opponent until the last-stretch drive. Somewhere in the last 50 meters you can summon all your strength and burst past him before he can recover from his surprise.

In extreme cases you might time your burst for the last 10 meters. Sometimes a runner lets down a meter or so before the finish line. Jazy did so in the 1964 Olympic 5000 and it cost him the bronze medal. If he had known Dellinger could pass him in the last two meters he would never have let down.

And so, if you struggled alongside 50 meters from the end you still might lose. If you have only one small burst in reserve it might win for you by holding it to the very end. The combination of your slight increase and his slight letdown might win for you. This is an extreme measure, of course, used only when you cannot win in any other way.

All these tactical points should be in your head, ready for use when the opportunity arises. When you are fatigued you cannot think clearly, and so you must do your thinking before the race.

This is done by planning. Taking into account the whole situation, you decide upon your ideal pace. Start by deciding your best pace if you were running alone. Then modify it to fit your present condition, the physical conditions of the track and weather, your opponents' habitual tactics, and your starting lane.

Next, decide the conditions under which you will run faster or slower than this pace. Is it worth it to you to run half a second faster per lap to stay with the leader? How much will you spend to take the lead on the last lap?

Then consider all possible situations. Imagine yourself in each position at each stage of the race at each of several different paces. What do you do in each situation? If you have made these decisions while you are rested and thinking clearly, and if you have gone over them enough to impress them upon your memory, then you will probably make the right move during the race.

It is like having a computer give you the answer instantly for each situation. If you used a computer, you would have to program it first with all the answers. You can do exactly the same thing without the computer. The only problem is making your body respond to what your mind knows is best.

Herb Elliott did this in a picturesque way. He trained himself to respond to the bell for the last lap by saying, "Ding-a-ling-a-ling" in training just before he launched into a simulated last-lap drive.

Go over all these possibilities again and again so that you are programmed to respond in the right way. Then you will defeat more than your share of your opponents and you will be known as a great tactician. And you will not waste any of the energy you have developed in your training.

References

1 Ahlborg, Bjorn et al, "Muscle Glycogen and Muscle Electrolytes During Prolonged Physical Exercise," *Acta. Physiologica Scandinavica,* v. 70, June 1967.

2 Asmussen, Erling, "Muscular Exercise," *Handbook of Physiology,* Sec 2, v. II, American Physiological Society, Washington D.C., 1965.

3 Asmussen, Erling, "Muscular Exercise," *Handbook of Physiology,* Sec. 3, Respiration, v. II, American Physiological Society, Washington D.C., 1965.

4 Astrand, Per-Olaf, M.D. and Rodahl, Kaare, M.D., *Textbook of Work Physiology,* McGraw-Hill Book Co., New York, 1970.

5 Astrand et al, "Cardiac Output During Submaximal and Maximal Work," *Journal of Applied Physiology,* v. 19, 1964.

6 Astrand, P-O, *Canadian Medical Association Journal,* March 25, 1967.

7 Astrand, P-O, "Concluding Remarks," *Canadian Medical Association Journal,* March 25, 1967, p. 907.

8 Bader, Hermann, "The Anatomy and Physiology of the Vascular Wall," *Handbook of Physiology,* Sec. 2, v. II, Circulation. American Physiological Society, Washington D.C., 1962.

9 Bailey, Herbert, *Vitamin E, Your Key To A Healthy Heart,* ARC Books, Inc., New York, 1964.

10 Bean, W.B. et al, *Proceedings of the Society of Experimental Biological Medicine,* v. 86, 1954, p. 693.

183

11 Bergstrom, Jonas and Hultman, Eric, *Nature,* April 16, 1966, p. 310.

12 Berman, William, *Beginning Biochemistry,* Sentinel Book Publishers, Inc., New York, 1968.

13 Bogert, L. Jean, *Nutrition and Physical Fitness,* W.B. Saunders Co., Philadelphia, 3rd ed., 1940.

14 Bork, John, "Mihaly Igloi: The Man and the Coach," *Track Technique,* No. 18, *Track & Field News,* Los Altos, Calif., December 1964.

15 Bowerman, Bill, "The Oregon School of Running," *Track & Field Clinic Notes,* National Collegiate Track Coaches Association, Ann Arbor, Mich., 1961.

16 Brown, Dr. G.O., "Blood Destruction During Exercise," *Journal of Experimental Medicine,* v. 36, 1922, p. 481 and v. 37, 1923, p. 113.

17 Carlile, Forbes, "Athlete and Adaptation to Stress," *Run Run Run, Track & Field News,* Los Altos, Calif., 1964.

18 Carlson, Lars A. and Pernow, Bengt, "Studies on the Peripheral Circulation and Metabolism in Man," *Acta. Physiologica Scandinavica,* v. 52, 1961.

19 Carman, Bob, *Distance Running News,* Manhattan, Kan., March 1969.

20 Carter, Larry, "Athletic Injuries," *Senior T.C. Newsletter,* v. 2, No. 10. Reprinted in *The Runner's World,* Mountain View, Calif., January 1970.

21 Cerutty, Percy, *Running With Cerutty, Track & Field News,* Los Altos, Calif., 1959.

22 Coker, Chuck, "Diet and Training Tips for Athletes," *Track & Field Clinic Notes,* National Collegiate Track Coaches Association, Ann Arbor, Mich., 1958.

23 Costill, Dr. David L., *What Research Tells the Coach About Distance Running,* American Association for Health, Physical Education, and Recreation, Washington D.C., 1968.

24 Costill, Dr. David L., "To Drink or Not To Drink," *Distance Running News,* Manhattan, Kan., September 1969.

25 Costill, Dr. David L., "Championship Material," *Runner's World* magazine, April 1974.

26 Counsilman, James E., *The Science of Swimming,* Prentice-Hall, Inc., Englewood Cliffs, N.J., 1968.

27 Coyne, W.N., "Notes of Steeplechasing," *Coaching Newsletter,* No. 8, July 1958, p. 8.

28 Daniels, J.T., *Ph.D. Dissertation,* The University of Wisconsin, January 1969.

29 Darden, Ellington, Ph.D., "Strong Points On Weight Training," *Runner's World* magazine, December 1975, p. 40.

30 Davis, Adelle, *Let's Get Well,* Harcourt, Brace & World, Inc., New York, 1965.

31 Day, P.L. et al, *Federation Proceedings,* v. 15, 1956, p. 548.

32 Dill, David B., "Physiological Adjustments of Altitude Changes," *Journal of the American Medical Association,* September 9, 1968.

33 Dobbs, Tad, Personal communication, December 1969.

34 Doherty, J. Kenneth, *Modern Training for Running,* Prentice-Hall, Inc., Englewood Cliffs, N.J., 1964.

35 Down, Michael Geoffrey, "An Appraisal of Interval Training," *Track Technique*, No. 25, *Track & Field News,* Los Altos, Calif., September 1966.

36 Dugal, L.P. et al, *Endocrinology,* v. 44, 1945, p. 420.

37 Edelen, Buddy, "Marathon Running," *Run Run Run, Track & Field News,* Los Altos, Calif., 1964.

38 Einstein, Albert B. ed., *The Adrenal Cortex,* Little, Brown, and Co., Boston, 1967.

39 Ekblom, Bjorn and Hermansen, Lars, "Cardiac Output in Athletes," *Journal of Applied Physiology,* v. 25, 1968.

40 Ekblom et al, "Effects of Training on Circulatory Response to Exercise," *Journal of Applied Physiology,* v. 24, 1968.

41 Ekblom, Bjorn et al, "Response to Exercise After Blood Loss and Reinfusion," *Journal of Applied Physiology,* v. 32, No. 2, August 1972.

42 Elson, Peter, "Strength Increases By Electrical Stimulation," *Track Technique,* No. 58, December 1974.

43 Eskamp, Robert, "Observations of Distance Running," *Track &*

Field Quarterly Review, National Collegiate Track Coaches Association, Ann Arbor, Mich., 1964.

44 Harris, Edmond J., "The Blood Picture of Athletes as Affected by Intercollegiate Sports," *American Journal of Anatomy,* v. 72, 1943.

45 Gordon et al, "Observations on a Group of Marathon Runners," *Archives of Internal Medicine,* v. 33, 1924, pp. 425-34.

46 Guild, Dr. Warren R., "Pre-Event Nutrition," *Track Technique* No. 2, *Track & Field News,* Los Altos, Calif., December 1960.

47 Hedman, Rune, "The Available Glycogen in Man and the Connection Between Rate of Oxygen Intake and Carbohydrate Usage," *Acta. Physiologica Scandinavica,* v. 40, 1957.

48 Henderson, Joe, *Long Slow Distance, Track & Field News,* Los Altos, Calif., 1970.

49 Herbert, V., *American Journal of Clinical Nutrition,* v. 12, 1963, p. 17.

50 Higdon, Hal, "Thoughts From the Coach of Coaches, Arthur Lydiard," *Runner's World* magazine, August 1977.

51 Hines, J.D. et al, *American Journal of Clinical Nutrition,* v. 14, 1964, p. 137.

52 Holloszy, John O., "Effects of Exercise on Mitochondrial Oxygen Uptake and Respiratory Enzyme Activity in Skeletal Muscle," *The Journal of Biological Chemistry,* v. 242, 1967.

53 Holman, Ron, "Anemia And The Athlete," *Athletics Weekly,* v. 21, London, October 28, 1967.

54 Horwitt, M.K. et al, *Federation Proceedings,* v. 17, 1958, p. 245.

55 Hurley, L.S. et al, *Journal of Biological Chemistry,* v. 195, 1952, p. 583.

56 Hyman, Martin and Tulloh, Bruce, *Long Distance Running,* Amateur Athletic Association, London, 1966.

57 Jacoby, Edward G., "Physiological Implications of Interval Training," *Track & Field Quarterly Review,* U.S. Track Coaches Association, Ann Arbor, Mich., March 1969.

58 Jensen Dr. Clayne R., "The Controversy of Warmup," *Quarterly Review,* U.S. Track Coaches Association, Ann Arbor, Mich., May 1968.

59 Jesse, John, "Weight Training For Runners," *Track & Field Quarterly Review,* National Collegiate Track Coaches Association, Ann Arbor, Mich., February 1964.

60 Jesse, John, "Weight Training For Running," *The Runner's World,* November 1969. Reprinted from *Modern Athlete and Coach,* London, November 1968.

61 Jobsis, Frans F., "Basic Process in Cellular Respiration," *Handbook of Physiology,* Sec. 3, Respiration, v. I, American Physiological Society, Washington, D.C.

62 Jokl, Dr. Ernest, *Physiology of Exercise,* Charles C. Thomas, Springfield, Ill., 1964.

63 Karikosk, O., "Training Young Middle Distance Runners," *Track Technique,* No. 66, December 1976, *Track & Field News,* Los Altos, Calif.

64 Karpovich, Dr. Peter V., *Physiology of Muscular Activity,* W.B. Saunders Co., Philadelphia, 5th ed., 1959.

65 Karvonen, M.J., "Effects of Vigorous Exercise on the Heart," *Work and the Heart,* Paul B. Hoeber, New York, 1959.

66 Kjellmer, Ingemar, "The Effect of Exercise on the Vascular Bed of Skeletal Muscle," *Acta. Physiologica Scandinavica,* v. 62, 1964.

67 Krehl, W.A. et al, *Borden's Review of Nutritional Research,* v. 24, 1963.

68 Krogh, August, *The Anatomy and Physiology of Capillaries,* Hafner Publishing Co., New York, 1959.

69 Krustev, Dr. Karstiu, "Oxygen and Sporting Achievement," *Bulletin D'Information,* Comite Olympique Bulgare, Sofia, 1963.

70 Kugelmass, I. Newton, *Biochemistry of Blood in Health and Disease,* Charles C. Thomas, Springfield, Ill., 1959.

71 Kuts, Vladimir, "Tactics in Long Distance Running," *Legkaya Athletika* No. 4, Moscow, 1961.

72 Landy, John, *How They Train, Track & Field News,* Los Altos, Calif., 1959, p. 24.

73 Lappe, Frances Moore, *Diet For A Small Planet,* Ballantine Books, New York, 1971.

74 Lavery, James A., "Achilles Tendon Injury Preventative Measures," *Track & Field Quarterly Review,* National Collegiate

Track Coaches Association, Ann Arbor, Mich., December, 1964.

75 Lawrence, Allan, "Australian Training," *How They Train, Track & Field News,* Los Altos, Calif., 1959.

76 LeMessurier, D.H., "Physiology of Altitude Acclimatization," *Track Technique,* No. 27, *Track & Field News,* Los Altos, Calif., March 1967.

77 Lydiard, Arthur, *Run To The Top,* Minerva Ltd., Auckland, N.Z., 1962.

78 MacIntyre, Dr. A.M.D., "Physiological Aspects of Training and Competition," *Track Technique* No. 32, *Track & Field News,* Los Altos, Calif., June 1969.

79 Margaria, Rodolfo, "Anaerobic Metabolism in Muscle," *Canadian Medical Association Journal,* v. 96, March 25, 1967.

80 Margaria, Rodolfo et al, "The Possible Mechanisms of Contracting and Paying the Oxygen Debt and the Role of Lactic Acid in Muscular Contraction," *American Journal of Physiology,* v. 106, 1933.

81 Margaria, Rodolfo et al, "Energy Cost of Running," *Journal of Applied Physiology,* v. 18, 1963.

82 Margaria, Rodolfo et al, "Energy Utilization in Intermittent Exercise of Supramaximal Intensity," *Journal of Applied Physiology,* v. 26, 1969.

83 Mitchell, *American Journal of Medical Science,* v. 107, 1894, p. 503.

84 Morehouse, Lawrence E. and Miller, Augustus T., Jr., *Physiology of Exercise,* C.V. Mosby Co., St. Louis, 1963.

85 Nelson, Cordner, *The Miler,* S.G. Phillips, New York, 1969.

86 Nelson, Cordner, "Swedes Alter Distance Training Rules," *Track & Field News,* March 1949.

87 Nelson, Cordner, "Track Talk," *Track & Field News,* November 1952.

88 Nelson, Cordner, *The Jim Ryun Story,* Tafnews Press, Los Altos, Calif., 1967.

89 Nelson, Cordner, *Track and Field: The Great Ones,* Pelham Books Ltd., London, 1970.

90 Nelson, Cordner and Quercetani, R.L., *Runners And Races: 1500/Mile,* Tafnews Press, Los Altos, Calif., 1973.

91 Nelson, Cordner, "Elliott Massacres Field," *Track & Field News,* September 1960, p. 7.

92 Nett, Toni, "Foot Plant in Running," *Track Technique*, No. 15, *Track & Field News,* Los Altos, Calif., March 1964.

93 Nett, Toni, "Continuous Running Training," *Run Run Run, Track & Field News,* Los Altos, Calif., 1964.

94 Nett, Toni, "Examination of Interval Training," *Run Run Run, Track & Field News,* Los Altos, Calif. 1964.

95 Nett, Toni, "Complex Training," *Run Run Run, Track & Field News,* Los Altos, Calif., 1964.

96 Noon, Tom, "Effects of Speed and Overdistance Training on Young Runners," *Track Technique* No. 21, *Track & Field News,* Los Altos, Calif., September 1965.

97 Osler, Thomas J., *The Conditioning of Distance Runners, Long Distance Log,* Woodbury, N.J., 1967.

98 Ozolin, N.G., *Developing Stamina in Athletes,* Moscow, 1959.

99 Pattengale et al, "Augmentation of Skeletal Muscle Myoglobin by a Program of Treadmill Running," *American Journal of Physiology,* v. 213, No. 3, September 1967.

100 Powell, John T., "Basic Mechanical Principles of Running," *Track Technique*, No. 1, *Track & Field News,* Los Altos, Calif., September 1960.

101 Prokop, Dave, "Jerome Drayton," *The Runner's World,* Mountain View, Calif., March 1970.

102 Prokop, Dave, "Marty Liquori," *The Runner's World,* Mountain View, Calif., May, 1970, p. 12.

103 Pugh, L.G.C.E. et al, "Rectal Temperature, Weight Losses, and Sweat Rates in Marathon Running," *Journal of Applied Physiology,* v. 23, 1967.

104 Quercetani, Roberto, Personal communication, March, 1970.

105 Rankin, Dave, Personal communication.

106 Reindell, H., Roskamm, H., and Gerschler, W., *Intervalltraining,* Johann Ambrosius Barth, Munich, 1962.

107 Robinson, Sid, "Physiological Consideration of Pace in Running Middle Distance Races," *Clinic Notes, International Track and Field Digest,* 1956, pp. 219-24.

108 Rompotti, Major Kalevi, "Blood Test as a Guide to Training," *Run Run Run, Track & Field News,* Los Altos, Calif., 1964.

109 Rosandich, Thomas P., "The American Method of Distance Running," *Distance Running News,* Manhattan, Kan., September 1969.

110 Rosenkrantz, H.J., *Journal of Biological Chemistry,* v. 223, 1956, p. 47, and v. 224, 1957, p. 165.

111 Roskamm, Dr. H. et al, "Physiological Fundamentals of Training Methods," *Run Run Run, Track & Field News,* Los Altos, Calif., 1964.

112 Roskamm, Dr. H., "Optimum Patterns of Exercise for Healthy Adults," *Canadian Medical Association Journal,* v. 96, March 25, 1967.

113 Rowell, Loring B. et al, "Splanchnic Removal of Lactate and Pyruvate During Prolonged Exercise in Man," *Journal of Applied Physiology,* v. 21, 1966.

114 Rushmer, Robert F. and Smith, Orville A., Jr., "Cardiac Control," *Physiological Review,* v. 39, 1960.

115 Sacks, Jacob, "Recovery from Muscular Activity and Its Bearing on the Chemistry of Contraction," *American Journal of Physiology,* v. 122, 1938.

116 Saltin, Bengt and Hermansen, L., "Aerobic Work Capacity and Circulation at Exercise in Man," *Acta. Physiologica Scandinovica,* v. 62, Supplement: 230, 1964.

117 Sandwick, Charles M., "Pacing Machine," *Athletic Journal,* 47:1967.

118 Saunders, Tony, "Steeplechase Technique and Training," *Track Technique*, No. 35, *Track & Field News,* Los Altos, Calif., 1969.

119 Schade, Herbert, "Herbert Schade's Training Methods," *Run Run Run, Track & Field News,* Los Altos, Calif., 1964.

120 Schorez, Pavel, "The Extent and Intensity of Long Distance Training," *Legkaya Atletika,* v. 6, Moscow, June 1968.

121 Schulman, M.D. et al, *Journal of Biological Chemistry,* v. 226, 1957, p. 181.

122 Selye, Hans, *The Stress of Life,* McGraw-Hill Book Co., New York, 1956.

123 Sheehan, George, M.D., "Medical Advice," *Runner's World* magazine, August, 1977, p. 21.

124 Shils, M.E., *American Journal of Clinical Nutrition,* v. 15, 1964, p. 133.

125 Shute, Dr. Evan, "The Current Status of Alpha Tocopherol in Cardiovascular Disease," *The Summary,* December, 1959.

126 Sjostrand, Torgny, "Blood Volume," *Handbook of Physiology,* Sec. 2, v. 1, *American Physiological Society,* Washington, D.C., 1962.

127 Smith, Christanna and Kumpf, Karharine F., "The Effect of Exercise on Human Erythrocytes," *American Journal of the Medical Sciences,* v. 184, 1932.

128 Snell, Peter and Gilmour, Garth, *No Bugles No Drums,* Minerva Ltd., Auckland, N.Z., 1965.

129 Spindler, John, "The Physiological Basis of Interval Training," *Quarterly Review,* U.S. Track Coaches Association, Ann Arbor, Mich., March 1967.

130 Stephens, Dave, Personal communication to Joe Galli, 1955.

131 Taylor, H.L. et al, "The Effect of Sodium Chloride. . .," *American Journal of Physiology,* v. 140, 1943, p. 439.

132 Travers, P.R., "Muscle Fatigue and its Relationship to Injury," *Track Technique* No. 10, *Track & Field News,* Los Altos, Calif. December 1962.

133 Tui, C., *Journal of Clinical Nutrition,* v. 1, 1953, p. 232.

134 Ulrich, Celeste, "Stress and Sport," *Science and Medicine of Exercise and Sports,* Harper & Row, New York, 1960.

135 Valberg, L.S. et al, *British Journal of Nutrition,* v. 15, 1961, p. 473.

136 Van Aaken, Ernst, "Speed Through Endurance," *Athletics Weekly,* London, April 27, 1968.

137 Van Aaken, Ernst, M.D., and Berben, D., "The Waldniel Pure Endurance Method and Its Justification," *Track Technique,* in preparation.

138 Van Liere, E. et al, "Differences in Cardiac Hypertrophy in Exercise and Hypoxia," *Circulation Research,* v. 16, 1965.

139 Ward, Tony, "Modern Concepts of Middle Distance

Training," *Track Technique* No. 30, *Track & Field News,* Los Altos, Calif.

140 Wilt, Fred, "Training Talk," *How They Train, Track & Field News,* Los Altos, Calif., 1959.

141 Wilt, Fred, "Language of Training," *Run Run Run, Track & Field News,* Los Altos, Calif. 1964.

142 Wilt, Fred, "Training Tips and Points to Ponder," *Run Run Run.*

143 Wilt, Fred, "A Crash Program For Training Schoolboys," *Run Run Run.*

144 Wilt, Fred, "Derek Clayton — How He Trains," *Track Technique* No. 32, *Track & Field News,* Los Altos, Calif., June 1968.

145 Wintrobe, Dr. Maxwell M., *Clinical Hematology,* Lea and Febizer, Philadelphia, 1967.

146 Yakovlev, N.N., "Nutrition of the Athlete," *Track Technique* No. 20-26, *Track & Field News,* Los Altos, Calif. 1965-66.

147 Young, George, Personal communication, September 1969.

148 Zierler, M. et al, *Annals of New York Academy of Science,* v. 52, 1949, p. 180.

149 Zweifach, Dr. Benjamin, *Science News Letter,* July 24, 1965, p. 56.